Professional Telesales

Tony Pearson

authorHOUSE®

AuthorHouse™ UK Ltd.
500 Avebury Boulevard
Central Milton Keynes, MK9 2BE
www.authorhouse.co.uk
Phone: 08001974150

First published by AuthorHouse 5/27/2009

ISBN: 978-1-4389-7715-7 (sc)

This book is printed on acid-free paper.

Contents

How to use this book...VII

Introduction

Introduction.. 1
Customer Focused Sales... 5
Inbound and Outbound Telesales........................... 8

Section A - The First Call

Section A – The First Call 13
1.0 Introductions 13
   Your personal introduction.............................. 13
   Politeness & Patience 18
   Clarity 20
   The Enquiry 21
   Voicemail Introductions.................................... 23
   Business to Customer Introductions................. 25
   Inbound Introductions....................................... 26
2.0 Gate Keepers 27
   Get them on your side! 27
   Leading 28
3.0 First Call Aims 32
4.0 Introductory Information
(Marketing Materials).. 34
   Sales versus Marketing...................................... 36
   Email & Mail Introductions................................ 37
5.0 Organising your data 40
   Groups & qualification....................................... 40
   Suspects.. 40
   Prospects 41
   Pipeline... 42

Weighted Projections 43

Clients... 44

Excludes.. 44

Referees.. 45

6.0 The Sales process flow chart 46

Data Capture 48

Notes 50

Inbound data capture............................ 52

Section B - The Follow Up Call

Section B – The Follow Up Call 55

7.0 Establishing the Customers Needs 57

Inbound – assessing customer needs.......... 59

8.0 Questions 60

Open Questions.................................... 61

Fact-finding Questions.......................... 64

Closing Questions 65

Questioning techniques flow chart 68

9.0 Rapport.. 69

Safe Bets 71

Unsafe areas 72

Current Events 72

Geography 73

Key interest.. 74

Active listening 75

Positive Language 77

Weasel Words....................................... 79

10.0 Product Knowledge 80

Product knowledge............................... 81

Sector knowledge................................. 83

Competitors... 84

11.0 USP's, Features & Benefits 86

USP's.. 88

Features...89

Benefits 90

12.0 Meeting Customer's Needs 92

13.0 Buying signals 93

14.0 Opportunity spotting.....................................97

Objections/concerns 98

Competitors...99

Direct competition. 99

Indirect competition 100

Competitor SWOT analysis 100

Long term opportunities 103

Referrals 105

Calling a Referred Lead............................107

Section C - Getting Down To Business

Section C – Getting Down to Business.................111

15.0 The Sales Presentation 111

16.0 Appointment Setting 113

Get it 'pencilled' in 114

Meeting brief..115

Customer Focused Sales checkpoint 4 19

Inbound lead generation 120

17.0 Closing techniques..121

Multiple Choice closing 122

Presumptive closing 123

Customer agreement..125

Fear of loss 125

Return on Investment......................................126

Two-way Street..127

Easy-in Easy-out..128

Section D - You The Sales Person

Section D – You the salesperson............................ 133
18.0 Keeping a customer on the phone 133
19.0 Motivation.. 134
20.0 Quality versus Quantity................................ 138
21.0 Scripting.. 139
　　　Natural Language 142
Conclusion - The Business Relationship................ 143

Appendix

Summary of Top Tips... 147
Things to discuss with your line
manager/colleagues.. 155
Sales Articles... 158
About the Author &
Where this book comes from. 163

Foreword

Nadio Granata – Senior Lecturer, Company Director, Chartered Marketer

Professional Telesales takes the reader on a journey which, quite frankly, I wish I had been fortunate enough to make many years ago when starting out in business myself. Speaking as a Chartered Marketer, it is fair to say that I am often uncomfortable about the impression that telesales can have on the marketing industry – all too often that annoying teatime disruption is referred to as a 'marketing call' and leaves all concerned quite hacked off for answering the call. We've all been there!

But relief is on the way ...

By working one's way through this no-nonsense, non-scientific approach to effective telesales calling, both the caller and the unsuspecting customer will be spared the anguish of irrelevance and instead be engaged by a meaningful and worthwhile conversation. Barriers will fall. Common ground will appear. Goals will be achieved. Sales will most definitely be made.

I congratulate Tony Pearson on his thorough and yet concise description of the world of telesales and expect to hear much more about the new breed of empowered, confident generation of telemarketers on whom so much of a business's success depends.

©Nadio Granata 8th March 2009

How to use this book

I have laid out all the text in sections and chapters that progress as you would expect a sales call to. A full key is at the beginning of this book so that you can easily refer back to any section at a later date. Any section or chapter can be read in isolation so please read this book and come back to any areas of interest later to further help increase your own ideas to improve your calling.

Section A discusses your introduction to a phone call, levels of professionalism and how to categorise and develop your contact information. A lot of sales calls fall down very early so this is a key stage in developing the number of calls, which begin and develop in a more successful way.

Section B looks at how you begin to develop those companies or people who have expressed an initial interest in what you are selling by looking at questioning techniques, rapport building product knowledge, meeting customer requirements and how to structure your sales presentation.

Section C is concerned with getting people to sign on the dotted line so to speak. There are lots of ideas in this section about how to get a commitment from your customer whatever your desired outcome is.

Section D covers those auxiliary functions of telesales that aren't you speaking to your customer directly. Other concerns that can arise when you work in telesales regarding confidence, motivation, structure and so forth.

At different intervals I make suggestions of things that you might want to discuss with your line manager or appropriate colleagues. These, along with the top tips raised throughout the book are summarised in the *Appendix*.

This book should provide you with lots of new ways of thinking about your sales approach. I do not assume that you do everything badly at the moment and that you should stop what you are doing and do exactly as I suggest in this book. Instead, I encourage you to take ideas from this book, share them with colleagues and combine them with your own existing ideas and practices in order to improve where you can and achieve better results. If you are relatively new to performing telesales activities I sincerely hope that this book gives you a great platform to begin from and wish you all much success.

Many of the skills covered are not isolated to telesales, they can also be used face-to-face, though there are no fashion tips included!

It won't be the last time you read these two words but.... Happy Selling!

Introduction

Introduction

'Professional telesales' might seem like a contradiction in terms to some people. Sales calls can be irritating and unprofessional, we've all experienced it as consumers but it is a fact that telesales is one of the strongest forms of marketing available to a company and that's why so many companies use telesales. Have you ever bought from someone over the phone or at least stopped to listen to what they were saying? At home or at work? I'm certain you have. I know I have. I'm sure you're a lot like me, very often you'll politely explain that you're 'not interested' and hang up but now and again you'll have a much longer conversation where someone actually manages to capture your interest over the phone. True? The reason that some of the calls you receive last a lot longer and some not so long, other than when someone calls you when you have your hands full, is due to the caller's sales techniques. How they introduce themselves, what questions they ask, their manner, whether they listen to you and talk to you about you or just reel off a script, how appropriate what they have to sell is to you and so on. Without realising it you talk to the best *sales* people for longer, much longer.

Approximately 57,000 people in the UK are full time telesales people. Combine this with overseas call centres and other business owners/workers whose duties include some aspect of sales and it can be difficult to stand out from the crowd.

'Sales' (along with 'marketing' and 'advertising') as a word can often get people's backs up. No-one likes to think that they're being sold to. They like to think that they only buy, when they want to buy and rightly so. Who has the right to call you and tell you what you need or force something upon you? No-one.

Sales is not about tricking people into paying money for something, it is not solely a competition to see who can make the most money. The best sales people are 'people people'. People who want to help their customers, build relationships, save people money, provide people with benefits. A good sales person cares about their customer and the quality of the products they buy or the standard of service they receive. They put the customer first and do everything they can to meet that customer's requirements. If that customer cannot be helped by the services that they provide, they do not try to sell them something anyway. A good sales person recommends the best thing for the client, even if it misses a sales right there and then because that honest approach will lead to future business from referrals etc. A good sales person asks dozens of questions before he/she makes a recommendation to a customer or tailors a quote or books an appointment.

All too often these principles of sales are missing in telesales. Whether it is something that can be ordered over the phone or business-to-business companies looking to book sales appointments, the script is set and the call centre worker makes call after call, reading the script again and again, verbatim and achieving little except annoying people at the other end of the phone. This reversion to the 'numbers game' is what gives the job a poor reputation not to mention results in many missed opportunities.

In this book we are going to go through all the essential aspects of a business to business sales call. These techniques are applicable whether you are selling over the phone, booking appointments or just generating leads and business relationships.

I know that sometimes people will slam the phone down on you before you've had the chance to tell them you're selling bars of gold for £1.50 and that sometimes people will be just rude for no reason. That's telesales and that will always occur now and again but you can make it less and less frequent and get more conversations going, longer and more productive conversations, which yield results.

A lot of business help books talk you though a fictional company example that runs perfectly all the way through. I find these types of books a little patronising, because let's face it, there's probably no such thing as a *perfect* call, so this book is just me talking you through different areas of a sales call with some basic examples of what you might use. There are no 'tricks' in this book, just lots of good ideas. I cannot and would not describe ways of pulling the wool over people's eyes or ways of making pigs wear lipstick (it's still a pig!). This book is a simply full of ideas to help you reconsider each aspect of your telephone sales abilities and hopefully make a few improvements. If anything comes across as obvious or patronising, that is not my intention. I am simply writing for an open audience and you may be more experienced than the next reader.

Are you currently a good sales person? I hope you answer 'yes' to this and you probably have done because it's always the good sales people who want to improve, who are hungry to succeed and get results, for you, your employer and your customer and if you're reading this book, you're obviously looking to improve and succeed. This is a book of suggestions from an experienced telesales manager of things that could improve your calling. These skills and ideas are applicable if you sell financial services, security, logistics, web-design, media services, medical or pharmaceutical services, advertising, health and safety services, recruitment, catering, telecoms, office supplies and so on and so forth. I have seen these skills vastly improve results in all of those sectors and more beyond that.

Just a couple of quick notes here, one to say that I refer to a potential client as the 'customer' throughout this book, simply because I find it a bit more personable than constantly referring to them as 'suspects' or 'prospects'. I will refer to people who already buy from you as 'clients'. And two, there are a few examples of sales techniques that I give where I talk about face-to-face sales. This is mainly where I get you to think about being the customer to try and get you to look at these techniques in a new way, rather than because they are just face-to-face techniques. All the techniques in this book are aimed at making you more effective *on the phone.* And speaking of thinking about the customer...

Customer Focused Sales

The theory you will find as a theme throughout this book is what I term, 'Customer Focused Sales'. This is a method of selling that gets away from the numbers game approach and the pushy sales person that everyone hates to come across, the, 'you've got to listen to me I know what you need' approach.

This is a method of selling where you do your upmost to appreciate the customer's position and try to understand their needs as best you can and then tailor your sales approach to meet the needs of your customer.

Recall a time when you have been irritated by a sales person. Why was it that they annoyed you?

Recall a time when you came across a sales person that was good. What made you buy from them?

Though everyone will have their own story to tell, I would wager a good bet that the sales person you didn't like was a combination of pushy, in your face, didn't want to give you time to think, kept on talking, correcting you and so on. I also bet that thinking of a time when someone was a good sales person was a lot more difficult to recall. The reason for this is that no-one likes to feel that they are being sold to and the good sales person doesn't make you feel like you're being sold to. They make it your decision to buy. If you walk into a shop and choose an item and take it to the till, you don't feel like you've been sold to, you know it was your decision. You have come across sales people in you experience as a customer that have sold to you without you feeling like you're being sold to. This is not because they perform some kind of mind-trick on you, it is because they find out precisely what would meet your needs before they sell you anything. Then when you've identified what you would be interested in, they then offer it you and wah-la! You've bought.

Performing customer focused sales pro-actively over the telephone is slightly more difficult. There are other hurdles to overcome as well as making your products and services meet the needs of your client. This book will address all of those issues too but I can assure you that being a customer focused sales person is very achievable, even as a lead generator or telesales person. Rather than always thinking, 'what should I say and how should I say it?', reverse the process and try to think, 'If I was the customer, what would I be looking for? How would I feel about this?' And so on.

To check if you are already a customer focused sales person (and you might well be, this book isn't here to change you, it's here to give you more ideas and tips) ask yourself this. If I didn't really have something that suited the customer, would I tell them so and make alternative suggestions or would I try and sell them something anyway? Being willing to pass up the opportunity to try and sell something if there isn't a match, doesn't make you a poor sales person, it just means that you put your customer first, which as an overall strategy will get you more, good quality sales, repeat business and great referrals. If you find yourself doing this too often, it might be you avoiding closing deals or you might need to re-address your target audience or services! I'm sure you'll find that this approach will mean for every hard-nosed sale opportunity you will pass up, you will get a great number of additional sales. And no, I do not encourage you to actively seek out opportunities to pass up business, it's just that this will inevitably occur.

You might think of it as good customer service starting very early. You know that where you experience good customer service, you buy from again and tell friends, family and colleagues about. This positive experience can start from the very first call with you, the telesales person.

Throughout this book we will look at ways to build a conversations that produces excellent sales results, leading to great business relationships that will feed your business long term. We'll also have a few checkpoints in order to revisit Customer Focused Sales and discuss how this fits into the calling.

Inbound and Outbound Telesales

This book is geared towards an outbound telephone call, from the initial introduction right through to closing the deal and beyond. If you work on an inbound sales team, receiving calls rather than making them, the majority of these techniques are still very much applicable to you. Yes, you might not have to introduce the company in the same way. If you're customer has phoned you, they're probably well aware of who you (the company) are and what you do. You're also possibly more aware of the benefits of being customer focused to help you achieve sales, if you're handling enquiries before you make sales, you'll know that the more helpful you've been to the customer throughout the call, the more likely you are to get a sale. There are also many more techniques in this book which will increase your conversion rates.

Many of the inbound telesales people I've worked with have been particularly good at the customer service side of the job but feel a lot less comfortable when it comes to making a sales presentation to the customer, usually towards the end of the call. They go from being controlled and confident when dealing with an enquiry into rushing and pessimistic when attempting a sales pitch. Some have said to me that they consider themselves to be very good at customer services and very poor at sales. I think that this makes little sense as the two roles are so interlinked. A lot of this doubt has to do with confidence issues and identifying what is actually expected of you as a sales person.

If you were on the phone to your bank and mentioned that you had a credit card elsewhere that you were paying 17.9% APR on and the person who were speaking to said that they were currently offering 0% on balance transfers for 12 months with a 2.5% fee, then reverting to 14.9% (i.e. they were a lot cheaper) and asked you if you would like to make an application because if you were successful, you would definitely be saving money. Is this sales or just very good customer service? The line isn't always this thin but if you're good at listening to your customer and considering their needs then you're half way to being a very successful sales person.

During the book I will make additional notes in certain chapters that are specific for those of you working on an inbound line, though you should be able to draw ideas from every single chapter of the book. If I do imply anything negative about call centres it is purely because of the typical ideas people who have never worked in a call centre have of them. I have worked in call centres and seen the good, the bad, the ugly and the fantastic but the stereotype is unfortunately poor. So, if it is a call centre environment that you work in, this book will help you break that poor image and be considered as professional as the top sales people in the country.

Happy Selling!

Section A
The First Call

Section A – The First Call

1.0 Introductions

I suppose there's no better place to start than by looking at what is arguably one of the most important parts of your call - your introduction. Whether you are introducing your company on a cold call to a receptionist or introducing yourself to a decision maker of a good prospect, your introduction is vital in buying you more time to achieve your goals on that call and giving the person you are speaking to the right impression about you and your company.

1.1   Your personal introduction

Let's break your introduction down into components and look at an example for a first time call.

Here's a pretty poor example, that you may have heard used before, 'Hi, it's John from Jolly Rogers. Can I speak to someone who deals with your procurement please?' or even just, 'Can I speak to somebody who deals with your procurement please?' Have you ever picked the phone up to someone who has said something like this? How much do you want to get off the phone straight away? How unprofessional does this sound? Unfortunately, this structure is all too often used. It's impersonal, difficult to say naturally and cheerfully and completely dismisses the person to whom you are talking.

Let's try and improve it in stages by looking at each component of the introduction. Not every chapter will be looking at word by word usage for your calling but this is particularly useful for your introduction and getting you off on the right foot:

Your first utterance over the phone is your greeting, in the example above, simply a 'hi'. People mistake this for being good because it's informal and informality leads to rapport, informality and rapport are not mutually inclusive and in fact being informal has quite the reverse effect with someone you haven't spoken with previously (we'll be discussing professional ways to build rapport in much more detail later). The fact of the matter is that 'hi' makes you sound like an American teenager. Nothing against American teenagers, other than British business people would rather do business with other British business people, rather than be pestered at work by Hannah Montana.

Imagine the Chief Executive of a National Bank making a call to a business associate. What is he most likely to say? 'Hi', 'Hello' or 'Good morning/afternoon'? I would expect 'Good morning/afternoon'. It is positive language as it includes the word 'good' and sounds far more professional. Would you rather sound more like a bank's Chief Executive or a run of the mill call centre worker. You may well work in a call centre but you need to stand out and to do this you need to break the stereotypes and sound as professional and competent as possible.

Your second utterance is your name. Again imagine our CEO making a business call, how would he state his name? 'It's John' or 'My name is John Smith'. This latter of course (providing his name was John Smith!). The inclusion of a surname sounds simple but has a profound impact. Try it on your next few calls. Change between using both your first name and your surname and only using your first name when you first introduce yourself to someone over the phone. I have trialled this many times with different people and they have always found that, when using their surname, they are given more time on the phone, treated with more respect and taken more seriously. This is because you sound more professional to the customer. These very small changes, as you will continue to see throughout the book, will all add to your professional appearance. This is a perfect area to make a point about thinking of the customer rather than yourself. You may be put off using your surname because you might think you sound too pompous or as if you have an inflated sense of self importance. Stop thinking internally and think about how it sounds to who you're saying it to. The majority of people would agree that including your surname, wherever possible and appropriate sounds more professional.

In addition, saying 'my name is' gives the statement more clarity rather than just saying 'it's'. It is very important to break up the key elements of your introduction to maintain that clarity. They key elements are; your name, your company, what you do and what you want. Do not rush your introduction and ensure that all these elements are clearly stated in their own right. Not by shouting them or really emphasising them but by simply separating them in your introduction with a sufficient number of words as to give the person you're speaking to time to make a quick note. (Too many words and of course you'll put the customer off, not to mention, possibly sound a bit mad!).

Next it's your company's name. A large proportion of company names have an indication of what they do in the title 'Geoff's Plumbing' or 'Nora's Butty Shop'. Look back at the above introduction. What do Jolly Rogers do? Those who don't have the description in their name need to add a description soon after for the purposes of an introductory call. Keeping the customer guessing is definitely not a good start to a call. In this example, Jolly Rogers are a wholesale provider of auto parts and spares for cars, calling retailers who would stock such products.

The final part of the introduction is where you state what you're looking to do. All too often telesales people will just ask outright to speak to the decision maker by asking a closed question 'can I speak to someone who deals with...' whatever it is that they're calling about. We'll cover questioning techniques in more detail later, though I will point out here that this question can easily be answered with a 'no' and the last thing you want your customers first words to you to be is 'no'. It is also very dismissive of whoever you are speaking to. Subliminally you are saying, 'you are not the person I need to be speaking to', 'I'm in a rush', 'put me on to someone who can actually make a decision about something important'. Not a good start.

A much better approach to this part of the call would be to clearly state why you are calling and then ask specifically *who* would be best to speak to. The reason you should always clearly state why you are calling is that you will get much further by steering the conversation in this way and not having the person you are speaking to having to ask questions to extract information from you. 'Can I?' gets a 'yes/no', 'who?' gets a name. Something along the lines of, 'I'm calling to see if I could provide someone with one of our catalogues today. Who would I be best to speak to please?' Now, rather than dismissing the person who are speaking to, you are including them in the business discussion and asking them to make a recommendation as to who would be the best person to speak to. They may also then have a better idea of who you actually need to speak to. Not only this but you are asking them for help and therefore engaging them with your plight. Much, much more effective.

Let's combine those improvements to see what we now have:

'Good Morning, my name is John Smith calling from Jolly Rogers Auto-parts. We supply quality spares to automotive retailers. I am looking to find out more about the products you sell and possibly provide someone with one of our brochures today. Who would be best to speak to?' This is a near perfect template (nothing is ever 100% perfect) though you may not always be able to get all of this across on every call, bear in mind your reason for this template introduction as use as much of it as possible when making your initial call.

Compare that to the first sentence, 'Hi, its John from Jolly Rogers. Can I speak to someone who deals with your procurement please?' Imagine answering the phone at work and hearing this. What are your thoughts?

Now imagine answering the phone to caller number two, 'Good Morning, my name is John Smith calling from Jolly Rogers Auto-parts. We supply quality spares to automotive retailers. I am looking to find out more about the products you sell and possibly provide someone with one of our brochures today. Who would be best to speak to?' How different is the effect? How do the two callers make you feel? Who are you most likely to respond positively to? Who is most likely to achieve what they set out to achieve?

Thinking about the introduction you currently use, how does this differ? How many calls do you lose at this early stage, which could now go a step further? The wording of these first few lines is vital for grabbing someone's attention, sounding professional, gaining respect and building rapport. Though we haven't got a sale just yet!

1.2   Politeness & Patience

The reason it is a great idea to always explain who you are, where you're calling from, what you do and the reason for your call even though you are most likely not speaking to the decision makers, is to get whoever you are speaking to on your side. If you dismiss them as unimportant by keeping them in the dark you sound impolite, 'can I speak to someone who deals with...' and risk them trying to get you off the phone before you speak. If they understand why you are calling and what you are looking for they are more likely to be able to help you because you have included them in what you are doing. Also, how unprofessional (or stupid) do you sound when you ask, 'can I speak to the person who deals with your procurement please?' and the voice at the other end of the phone says, 'that's me'. Then you decide to start talking to them like a human being and it's already too late. If you ask 'who's best to speak to please?' they can say, 'me'. Nothing's lost and you've got the decision maker on the phone! And he/she has just heard you're nice professional introduction and know why you're calling!

Speak to everyone as if they own the company. Politely, professionally, patiently. You wouldn't like to be dismissed as 'just another cold caller' and so practice what you preach!

It is also very important to be patient with your approach. By this I mean, take the time to speak to anyone you have on the phone and don't be concerned if you end up speaking to 3 or 4 people before you get through to the decision maker. Use this time to gather information and build rapport. Always take the names of people you have spoken to even if you only use it in an example such as this, 'Hello Paul, I spoke to Sheila and she said that you would be the ideal person to speak to about auto-parts'. Any further rapport you build can also be useful. 'Hello Paul, Sheila was telling me how busy you were at the moment so thanks for taking the time to speak with me' etc.

A great example of this is if you find out that the decision maker is on holiday. Ask politely where they have gone before you offer to call back in a week or two and make a note of where they went. When you call back you can bring that into the conversation straight away, 'Hi Paul, how was Egypt?'. Who doesn't like to talk about their holidays? It's polite and shows that you've taken an interest in them and takes the edge of speaking to someone for the first time. Remember, we're trying to get away from the notion of a 'cold' call. We'll be discussing both note-making and rapport building in more detail later.

The key to standing out from the crowd when making a sales call could be information you gleam from a colleague of the decision maker, which can make you more familiar with that company and simply speed up the process of building rapport. Everyone on the other end of the phone is an ally, unless you choose to make them otherwise. Even those who sound as if they'd initially rather get you off the phone can supply you with very useful information if you are patient and polite enough with them.

1.3   Clarity

Clarity is very important. This is why during your introduction you fully explain the who, where, what and why of your call - to save them having to ask. If you look at the good example again you will also see that the sentences are very clearly structured:

'Good Morning, my name is John Smith calling from Jolly Rogers Auto-parts. We supply quality spares to automotive retailers. I am looking to find out more about the products you sell and possibly provide someone with one of our brochures today. Who would be best to speak to?'

Speak slowly and clearly on your introductions. A receptionist at the other end of the phone might be trying to make a quick note of who's calling, they might also be affected by background noise and you just might not be speaking clearly enough.

What is almost as bad as withholding the information, forcing the customer to ask for the information again, is not speaking clearly enough, forcing the customer to have to ask for the information again! Either way you can come across as suspicious or incompetent, though armed with this new introduction, you should have very few issues with this providing you are speaking clearly.

1.4   The Enquiry

You should always approach your first call much more as if you were making an enquiry than as if you intend to sell to each company. There are several reason for this but first I'll explain a little further about what I mean.

When a person answers a call at work it could be anything, a sales enquiry, a sales person, a colleague who's out of the office, the admin assistant's husband wondering what's for tea or something completely different. You should always make your first call as if you are making an enquiry, by that I mean no hard sell in the first instance. This will instantly switch off the person who answered the phone into thinking they have a cold caller on the other end of the phone rather than someone who is looking to establish the requirements of their company. The introduction above is very professional and will give you an extra few moments of the person who answered the phone's time versus a typical cold caller introduction. What you need to be thinking is, *does this company meet my requirements as a customer*, i.e. can they benefit from my products and services and are they in a position to buy etc? This will remind you that you have called to find out about and to listen to them, not to force them to listen to you. As you will see throughout this book, the more you learn about the customer, the more likely you are to sell and thus the more sales you will achieve throughout your calling.

Pragmatically speaking, this is often likely to come into play immediately after you have made your introduction. You have given the person you are speaking to, possibly a 'gatekeeper' who we'll learn more about shortly, the precise information about who you are, where you're from, what you do etc. This is not to say that the gatekeeper will immediately understand exactly who you would ideally need to speak to, particularly when you are calling a larger company. They will quite often ask to know even more specifically why you're calling.

Let's follow the above example through a little further. We've made the introduction again but on this occasion we've called a larger company; 'Good Morning, my name is John Smith calling from Jolly Rogers Auto-parts. We supply quality spares to automotive retailers. I am looking to find out more about the products you sell and possibly provide someone with one of our brochures today. Who would be best to speak to?'

The receptionist may well ask for more specifics, even if this is for her benefit in buying some more thinking time. Rather than just repeat yourself as the temptation might be to, you can detail your call as more of an enquiry. 'I'm looking to find out more about what you sell and see if you might benefit from having a look at one of our brochures to add to your current product range. Ideally I could do with speaking with the person who is in charge of your stock just to see if our products fit in with what you sell.' Or something along those lines. At this stage, your introduction has bought you the time to be very specific about what you need to achieve on that call and yet you have not come across as an anonymous sales person but instead a business person who's making an enquiry and taking an interest in what it is that the customer does. Not a bad start!

1.5   Voicemail Introductions

I have worked with people who make outbound telesales calls and shy away from leaving voicemails on the phone of the decision maker. I am always flabbergasted by this. People who call people for a living don't like to talk to machines! Either that or they cannot see the benefit of doing so. Either way, a huge opportunity is being forsaken.

Some sales people think that they shouldn't leave a voicemail because they aren't making an important call and therefore should simply call back later. If you don't think the call is of any importance then why on Earth should the customer consider it important? Let's again think of our Chief Executive making a call. If he was making the call that he earlier introduced so professionally but got through to the person's voicemail do you think that he would leave a message? Of course he would. Not only this but the message would be relevant, concise and professional much like his introduction.

Here's an example of how you can amend your introduction to be suitable for a voicemail message:

'Hello, this is a message for Paul Douglas. My name is John Smith calling from Jolly Rogers Auto-parts. We supply quality spares to automotive retailers. I was hoping to speak to you about the products you sell and to send you one of our brochures. I'll give you a try next week or you can reach me on 0208 9876 1234. That's John Smith from Jolly Rogers Autoparts on 0208 9876 1234. Many thanks'.

We have removed the 'good morning/afternoon' part as we don't know when they will next check their messages, so it's better to have this as neutral. We have still clearly stated our full name, where we're calling from and what we would like to discuss (i.e. the reason for the call).

I have included a key sentence here that you should double read the wording of as this is incredibly useful, 'I'll give you a try next week or you can reach me on 0208 9876 1234.' The reason that this is a crucial sentence is because if you just request a call back you could be waiting for that call for quite some time. Either that or you request a call back and because you don't get one call a busy person again a few days later, which could be construed as pestering. There again if you only say that you will call back and don't leave any contact details this prevent someone who is very keen to speak to your company having to wait for another call whilst their interest wanes or look unprofessional as the customer wonders why you were not comfortable leaving contact details. The combination of, 'I'll give you a try next week or you can reach me on 0208 9876 1234' is ideal because you may get a call back or you are free to make that second call.

Always repeat your name, company name and telephone number at the end of the call. If the customer was making a note of who called they may not have been able to get it all down first time so twice is ideal. Making someone replay your message to check your contact details because you only said them once isn't going to help your cause.

I'm sure that you would agree that any sales call you make is supported when the customer has heard of your company and/or is expecting your call. By leaving this message you have achieved both. The customer knows who you are, what you do and is expecting you to contact them at some stage. They are then far more likely to treat you as a professional, which will assist you achieving much longer and more productive calls. The sheer fact that you have left a message promotes the importance of the call from chance sales call to business discussion. Even if the result of the call is that when you next speak, whether they call you or you call back, is that they have another supplier that they are tied into or cannot use your services for another reason, you have maintained a very professional image and achieved all that you could have done.

Typically only a minor percentage of people who you leave a message for will call you back, however, those who do are more often than not those who have some sort of requirement that you may be able to address.

Always leave a voicemail if you have the opportunity - nothing to lose, plenty to gain.

1.6   Business to Customer Introductions

All this goes exactly the same if you are calling consumers at home rather than calling other companies. There's little that's more frustrating than being sat down for dinner when the phone goes and when you answer all you get is, 'are you the homeowner?' or 'can I speak to the person who pays for...' etc. Of course, calling people at home can be tricky but a professional introduction will massively soften the blow for the person at the other end of phone, who will take far more interest in what you are saying if a more appropriate greeting and introduction is employed.

This will be the only chapter specific to business to customer sales. There is nothing that needs to be done differently between calling companies and calling individuals, the only thing that differs is what you are selling.

1.7   Inbound Introductions

The introduction above is of course specifically aimed for an outbound call, though a lot of these principles are transferable to an inbound call. Very rarely when I call the bank, my mobile phone company, the electricity company etc, does anyone answer the phone with a full and professional introduction, which includes a surname.

People have an image of calling call centres and having little chance of speaking to anyone above the age of twenty. One, twenty year olds can be very helpful and professional. I worked in a call centre at nineteen years of age and would like to think that of myself and two, this is entirely inaccurate. I've been in several call centres doing training and met people of all ages. People sometimes associate the lack of professionalism with younger people. Consider including your surname when you take a call (whether you're twenty or fifty). This extra professionalism could take the edge of any complaint calls that you have to handle too, not to mention of course increasing the amount of respect your customer gives you when you start to mention those new offers you currently have!

2.0 Gate Keepers

Poor old receptionists get called quite a few names in this line of work and believe me when I say they call telesales people by much worse names! However, it needn't be this way. Receptionists, or colleagues of the person who are looking to speak to, can be your biggest ally, rather than your biggest blockade. I tend to use the phrase 'Gate Keeper' as this is a much fairer metaphoric image than the still mystical but somewhat nastier 'Dragon' label often associated with receptionists.

2.1   Get them on your side!

I've already highlighted the importance of fully introducing yourself to whoever may answer the phone as this is the first step to getting them on your side. However, there is more that you can do.

Think about being the person who answers the phone. We've already discussed the importance of your introduction and 'the three P's' of patience, professionalism and politeness and how differently that would make you act. Once you have won over the Gate Keeper in this way they can do two things for you:

1) Provide you with vital information such as:

- Your target contact's direct phone number and/or email address – this boosts the value of your data. The more contact information you have for each prospect, the more likely you are to sell to them.

- Information about their movements, i.e. when the best time to call back is – this is very useful with people who aren't heavily office based. It will save you a lot of time and of course in sales, as in business as a whole, time is money.

- Who the company uses for your type of services, when they are next due to review these services etc and other vital sales information that you can take into future calls – you need to establish the rapport first of all and then if they have the time to speak to you, get in a couple of questions before you end the call. Just because they are not the decision maker, does not mean that they don't know about the business they work in!

2) They might be able to put you through to the right person there and then and their manner in doing so can have a big effect. Imagine being at work and a colleague takes a call from someone who wants to speak to you. They hand you the phone with a stern expression and say, 'it's somebody, selling you something'. How will you feel when you pick the phone up? Of course you'll be looking to get them off the phone as quickly as possible. If they were to hand you the phone with a smile and say, 'It's John calling about a brochure for spares', you would be much more willing to have a discussion.

This could be the first time you've spoken to the decision maker but you can clearly see how much of a better footing you are on if you can win over their colleagues or 'Gate Keepers' (or Dragons!).

Rapport building is the other key part to this and we will look at rapport further in Section B.

2.2   Leading

Here's a little technique to vastly reduce the number of times people hang up on you. It can be very useful whether you are speaking to a gate-keeper, the decision maker or another colleague.

The truth of the matter is that very few people actually hang up on you. Very few indeed put the phone down regardless of what you are saying. Having a more effective introduction will in itself increase the number of people who are willing to listen to what you have to say, however, some may still consider you simply as a cold-caller and look to get you off the phone.

What tends to happen is that the person at the other end of the phone will try to speak very quickly and express a lack of interest. The caller will naturally match the pace of the person they are speaking to, rushing to get their point across and inadvertently accepting that they are being dismissed.

The best way to handle someone speaking quickly is not to match their pace but instead keep a steady pace and politely ask them more about their situation. This might not be as straight forward as it sounds but it's very effective. If you can maintain a relaxed pace and get them talking, they will begin to match you!

The main reason people want to rush you off the phone is because they are in the middle of their working day and haven't exactly been sat around waiting for your call so are likely very busy! Acknowledging this can help you grab a moment of their time, 'I appreciate that you're busy...' or 'I understand it might not be something you were looking at right now...' however, remember to maintain that pace! The slow and clear speech ,which you used during your introduction. These utterances will lose their effect if you are still rushing yourself. The result of this is that you sound more controlled and professional, allowing the conversation to develop. Of course the person you are calling may well be too busy to talk there and then but don't rush, just try and agree a time to call back even if you do get very little other information. The ideal way to ask is, 'when is the *best* time to call back?'. This shows that you fully appreciate their situation and that you want to operate on their terms. When you later call back and open with, 'Sorry I caught you while you were busy earlier', you will be off to a great start as they will remember how professional you sounded earlier and make more time for you.

This is actually a confidence issue. If you are confident enough that you have something that the customer will benefit from hearing about then you are much more likely to be able to hold your own when being slightly dismissed. If the person really is in a rush, the very least that you can achieve on that call is to again, maintain a steady pace and politely ask when a good time to call back would be as just suggested. Even if the answer is something vague such as, 'next week', you can thank them for their time and arrange the call back. When you then come to call back you can identify that they were very busy when you called last week and that you have called back as requested. You are already meeting a need of theirs. This is most likely a very familiar scenario to you but the key is to never be rushed off the phone by matching someone's accelerated pace. Maintain your own pace, stand your own ground. This will ultimately assist you in gaining the respect of the customer, providing you remain as polite as possible.

Customer Focus Sales – checkpoint 1

One of the first things to address as a telesales person, especially if you're new to telesales is the nerves you might feel when about to make a sales call and during its early stages. There's nothing embarrassing about this, everyone feels a twinge of nerves as they are about to make a call, it's as if you're giving a performance and it needs to go right. You might also feel under pressure because there's potentially a lot of money riding on each call. A lot of people, who unsurprisingly don't do sales for a living, couldn't imagine anything worse than having to make a cold call. I can't see what so nerve-racking about it but there again I couldn't imagine anything worse than laying bricks for a living and lots of people earn their living that way, so its each to their own I suppose.

The surprising thing is that a lot of telesales I have worked with, managed and trained seem to say the same things, which make them feel nervous. 'What if they're not interested', 'what if they're rude to me', 'what if they already have a provider' and so on. First of all I've always believed that a 'what if' kind of attitude is the least productive approach to life, regardless of what your job is (just a personal peeve!). Second people are rarely extremely rude to you on the phone and even when that does occur, what's the worst that could happen? I've never known anyone be killed over the phone...

Anyway, customer focused sales. When you receive a phone call how do you feel? Ready to be really nasty or just curious as to who it might be and what they might want? When someone does make a sales call to you, even if it

31

is something that you're really not interested in, do you shout a whole string of obscenities or just politely explain that you're not interested and the conversation ends? Exactly, the worst that could happen over the phone is that what you're selling is not applicable or of interest to the customer and therefore you'll move on to the next contact. No drama at all!

You're not nervous when you're on the phone to your friends, family, colleagues, existing customers or when someone's selling to you so there's no reason to be nervous when you're making a sales call. At the end of the day it's only another human being at the other end of the line, who you would not be nervous about speaking to face to face and if you ever feel those nerves just remind yourself of how you are when you receive a call and that should settle them for you.

3.0 First Call Aims

It is very rare that you will achieve a sale or book an appointment the first time you make contact with a company. This happens, and it's great when it does, though your main strategy should be to break this down across two types of call. You might make three or four calls or even more to achieve your sale/appointment but essentially you are making two different types of call, the introductory call and the follow up call (covered in sections A & B).

This being the case you should clearly outline your aims for your first call. Though these may vary from company to company and project to project, here are the types of basic elements to aim for a typical call one:

- Introduce the company (clearly and effectively as discussed above)

- Qualify that the customer falls into the category of your target market (i.e. they do what you thought they did – the data you are using will not always be 100% accurate).

- Confirm the decision maker's name and any additional contact details such as direct phone line, email or address if based from a different office.

- Speak to decision maker if available to introduce service.

- Agree to send further information via their preferred method (post or email).

- Agree to call back to discuss further when they have had a chance to review the information.

- Gain any other relevant information possible, current suppliers, due dates (though this begins to merge into the follow up call).

- Begin to build rapport.

- Find a hook – that is try and find something unique about that company to pick up on on your follow up call. This may be the holiday thing mentioned above, good rapport you have with a receptionist or equivalent, something specific about their company or requirements etc – something that means, when you call back you will be speaking specifically about them and starting on a warm foot (I don't know if a warm foot is a thing but hopefully you know what I mean).

Tony Pearson

- Make thorough notes of all the above.

If the person that you are after is not there you can still achieve all of the above points minus actually speaking to them. You can send across the information directly by email and still perform the follow up call knowing who you need to speak to and that they have received the information. You can then schedule a call for the appropriate time. It is important to try and gather as much information as possible and build rapport on the first call, otherwise your second call is still quite cold.

Though we are looking at this process as broken down into two calls, it will often be the case that you will make a few more than that. Sometimes the decision maker will not be available, sometimes they will want you to call back when they're less busy, sometimes they will want you to call back closer to the time when they will be reviewing those particular services etc. One aim always to have is, even on those short and sweet calls, to take one thing from each call that will benefit your next call from the example categories above, one more piece of contact information, one more piece of rapport etc.

4.0 Introductory Information (Marketing Materials)

I'm not going to go into too much detail about what you're introductory information should or shouldn't include or what format it's in as that's a discussion about marketing and here we're concentrating on sales. However, it's safe to assume that you will have some introductory information about your company, typically in formats such as a company brochure, flyer, letter, link to your website etc. There are however, a few things you should consider when sending your company information to a customer.

One is to make sure that the person receiving it knows it's coming. If you speak to someone and they ask for more information you can send it to them. When they then receive it, they are a lot less likely to throw it in the bin or consider it 'junk mail'. If you haven't had chance to speak to the decision maker and a colleague has asked you to send the information across, do you upmost to get that colleague to let the person you are after know that it is coming. If you don't manage this you are essentially sending them a mail-shot which is far more likely to find its way into the bin or being deleted and you're right back to square one.

Check your introductory letter. A template letter may not always suit each customer due to variations in their circumstances. Here's an example; sometimes companies write their introductions to follow up on a conversation and begin something along the lines of, 'Following our recent discussion...', this is fine so long as you have actually spoken to them. If you haven't, ensure that you amend the text accordingly. There are other elements of your template introductory information that might be laid out in this way. Each time you send some information scan the letter to ensure that it will make sense to the customer. Though it is unlikely to be the actual situation, an introductory letter should always read as if you wrote it after the call, specifically for that customer. The customer does not want to feel as if they are one of a hundred people you spoke to that day and that you are taking time over your communication with them.

Even if you are forwarding an email you might want to amend the text to make it more applicable to the person to whom you have spoken. Another example of this, similar to a letter, might be that near the end of the email your template says, 'I will contact you again in a few days time', no good if you've just agreed to call back in a month. Don't be lazy or rushed with emails, ensure each one is worded as applicable to that customer or once again, that professional image you have been working hard to build could be in jeopardy.

Particularly on emails, be careful with your spelling, layout, grammar etc. If in doubt, do not send and check with a colleague who you think has good writing skills. Sales abilities and writing abilities are two completely different things and there is no shame in being the top sales person, who still needs help with grammar!

The point here is that, it's no use being a customer focused sales person and then having your company information let you down.

4.1 Sales versus Marketing

Sales and marketing are of course lumped together on most occasions. As a telesales person you may not have any say in your marketing. Things such as your website, advertising, introductory letters, special offers, brochures and so on and so forth, may well just be dumped on your desk. For that reason I won't be making suggestions about what these should include.

Marketing is all the bumf (good word) that you have, which promotes the company, sales is you and the conversations you have with your customers and potential customers. Sales is key. Plenty of people buy from good sales people without ever coming across a piece of marketing material. I compare nice marketing, like a smart website or pretty brochure without the ability to close a deal to a Venus fly trap with lock-jaw. It's all a waste of time unless you can call your customer to action, which more often than not is down to the sales team.

4.2   Email & Mail Introductions

Nowadays, people often prefer to receive things by email, especially in the first instance as it's generally easier to deal with and a lot of businesses are very aware of the environmental issues surrounding post mailing.

Emails will also arrive much sooner so that the customer sees your company information whilst your first call is still fresh in their mind and you can make your follow up call much sooner. You can also add several things to emails, web-links, flyers etc, as well as easily amend your text, making emails very flexible.

Company brochures are useful to leave a good impression with your prospect but are altogether a lot more expensive per contact than email literature and so you might be costing your company quite a lot of money by sending out brochures to very basic prospects.

Both emails and postal literature may be requested to neutral contacts. i.e. if a company has a no name policy you might be asked to send a letter addressed to a position or a department or asked to send an email to a neutral address such as info@customer.com. If this is the case, simply pursue at the customer's pace, there's little more you can do.

If you do have a choice as to whether you send something out by email or through the post, always take your prospect's preference on this first and foremost. However, you may wish to consider the following points:

Method	Pros	Cons
Mail	• Can send out very professional materials • Literature can be kept on file for future reference • Can easily be handed between colleagues	• Expensive to produce & send • Rigid in terms of amending to meet your client's specific requirements • Can get lost in the post • Takes a few days to arrive • Easily binned • Damageable
Email	• Can be sent directly to the person you are speaking to within minutes • Practically free • Can be followed up on sooner • More environmentally friendly • Flexible to amend for each contact • Can be copied to more than one contact • Can easily be resent if not received or saved	• Up against spam filters • Any typo in an email address will be returned – may have to call company back and discuss (which doesn't look good) rather than postal service who cope with spelling errors all the time! • Amending email several times - more likely to include errors

Generally speaking I find its better to send emails, especially on the first call, as the above table shows all the benefits. Printed literature can then be saved for the strongest prospects or for face-to-face meetings. Field sales people always find it better to have something to leave the customer with, following an initial meeting.

5.0 Organising your data

We've reached the end of the first call, so I think that now would be a good time to look at how best to organise your data. Though I can give you no advice on the specific database, CRM or contact management system that you are using, this process will be compatible with them all.

Badly organised data will lose you business through, forgetting to collect vital information, not calling back at the right time, forgetting what has been previously discussed and lose you time through having to sift through your data each time you make a call.

5.1   Groups & qualification

You need to categorise your data to know roughly where you are with each contact so that you can move them along the sales pipeline until you secure business. Let's look at the categories:

5.2   Suspects

When you first purchase data and input this into your database you will just have basic contact information such as a name registered to the company, often with only a first initial, the company name and address and the main phone number. The name on the data is more often than not, not the person you need to speak to. You will have put these into your database because you *suspect* that they will have some requirement for your services, for instance a manufacturer of white boards might have a list of educational institutions to call. This data needs to be qualified.

What you are looking to do with suspects is to make them into a prospect. You do this by conducting your first call as described in detail, above. Identifying the decision maker & expanding the contact information, introducing your company and products/services, establishing the level of customers need (ensuring that they do indeed fall into your target market and may have some requirement for your products/services), and sending out information. If you tick these boxes, that contact may then be placed in the prospects group.

Turning suspects into prospects is the donkey work of telesales. I don't mean anything derogatory by that, I just mean that this is where you will be wading through a lot of similar calls, asking similar questions and often contacting companies that perhaps have no requirement for your services. Anyone who doesn't fit your customer profile for any reason is placed into the 'excludes' group (below). Things begin to become more fun when you're calling prospects.

5.3   Prospects

Prospects have been qualified as good potential customers for your business. You know who you should be speaking to, you know what they do and they've heard of you. i.e. they are who you are contacting on your follow up calls.

I consider the following to be a prospect:

- Full name of the decision maker

- Quality contact details – address, phone number and email address

- Fit customer profile, company size, location, sector etc

- Have expressed an interest in your services (i.e. requested further information or asked for call back)

- Introductory information has been sent

This list of prospects is your potential pot of gold. These are the people who you will do your upmost to build rapport with, understand their requirements and look to convert into business, usually via quotes, sales appointments or equivalent.

You are looking to either close a sale with these people or to book an appointment for one of your field sales staff to attend. On projects where you are looking to close a sale over the phone you are looking to move prospects into your 'clients' group. Those which require an appointment or quotation will be moved into the 'pipeline' group.

5.4   Pipeline

Your pipeline stores all the people you have discussed specific business with. You have either sent a quotation over the phone or by email or have booked an appointment for one of your sales people to attend. This does not include a generic price list. If you include a price list with your company information or someone asks to look at a price list that doesn't relate to a particular item or items then this is no different to the sort of information that you would send to a suspect when you were promoting them to a prospect. Only when a particular quote, such as what you would be able to gather face-to-face, is provided for that customer do you place them in the pipeline group.

If a field sales person has made a visit and is negotiating a contract or equivalent, the client remains in the pipeline until a sale is secured. As with prospects, contact in the pipeline can be moved to the excludes if the situation arises that means no sale can be secured.

Often, a field sales person will take over the relationship with the customer at this stage. If this is the case for you ensure that you gain regular updates on the situation so that you can keep the company's database up to date or do not contact the customer inappropriately.

5.5   Weighted Projections

Whilst in the pipeline you can rate each contact by their likelihood of conversion, based on your initial discussions over the phone and/or from feedback from the sales meeting. You can also keep tabs on how much you have quoted for and this allows you to do weighted projections across your pipeline. For instance, if you had quoted contact 1 for a contract at £1000 but thought you had a 75% chance of conversion your weighted projection would be £750. If you had quoted contact 2 for a contract for £2000 but thought you only had a 50% chance of conversion the weighted projection would be £1000. The total weighted projection is £1750, which is very useful if you're working this out across a higher number of contacts.

There is no precise way of calculating weighted projections, it is simply an estimate based on your discussions with each client, the stage of negoiations and your previous experience. Companies tend to work to 25% (25%, 50%, 75%) or 20% (20%, 40%, 60%, 80%) for their projections, rather than do anything overly precise. This helps with the financial projections of the company, helps you assess if you are meeting your targets and is a testing and measuring device so that you can look to improve your closing techniques (more on this later). A company only hits 100% when they've signed on the dotted line so to speak and at that stage they become a 'client'.

5.6   Clients
A client is simply, someone who has bought from you. It might have been a one off sale or an ongoing contract, or anything in between. Your clients are your revenue, not only this but there are also the best people to market to. As a sales person you are interested in securing more sales. You can gain repeat business and referral business from your clients (more on this later), which is actually the strongest way to get new leads and sales.

5.7   Excludes
Excludes are any contacts that you cannot sell to. This would include incorrect data that cannot be corrected online or elsewhere, contacts who have no requirement for your product or service or those who request to be taken off your list for one reason or another.

Those who declare that they just aren't interested in speaking to you because they perceive it as a sales call or without giving you a good reason you might leave in suspects and try a few months down the line. The word you are looking for is 'because'. You need to establish a reason that they don't want or can't use your services. This information can also be important for the long term growth of the business (i.e. ongoing market research).

If there is a permanent reason that a company will not/ cannot buy from you, place them in the excludes group so that they do not take up any more of your time. As much as we try to make the most of each contact we have and each person we speak to, sometimes companies will just not fit your customer profile for one reason or another and you are much better just moving on swiftly.

5.8   Referees

A referee may or may not be a client but promotes your services to their network. A client who is happy with your service may have one or more people you they can recommend to you. You might offer a discount to these clients or a referral commission.

For certain services you could also get your company on a preferred suppliers list. This often happens in the public sector. For instance, a local council will have a list of approved companies for each service they will source, which could lead to the local schools, hospitals and public funded buildings using our services (depending on what you sell of course!). These opportunities are also available in the private sector, particularly with blue chip companies.

Partnerships are also very effective when you share a target audience with another company. For instance, an insurance broker may have a strategic alliance with a company that provides mortgages, a web design might have a partnership with an IT support firm, a plumber might have a partnership with an electrician and so on. Anywhere the target audience is shared but the services are complimentary and not in any competition with one another. It might be worth looking at how many of these partnerships you currently have in place and considering the following:

- How effective are these referees? i.e. how much business do we get through them?

- When was the last time I spoke to them?

- What sectors/areas are these people in and are there any others that would be worth adding to this list?

You should market to or contact your referees as often as you do your prospects. Remind them of why they recommend you!

6.0 The Sales process flow chart

Here is a model to help you further understand the process broken down above. You will lose companies as you go through each stage (i.e. place them in the exclude group) but by understanding this process you will be able to maximise each call you make as you know precisely what your next aim for each customer is:

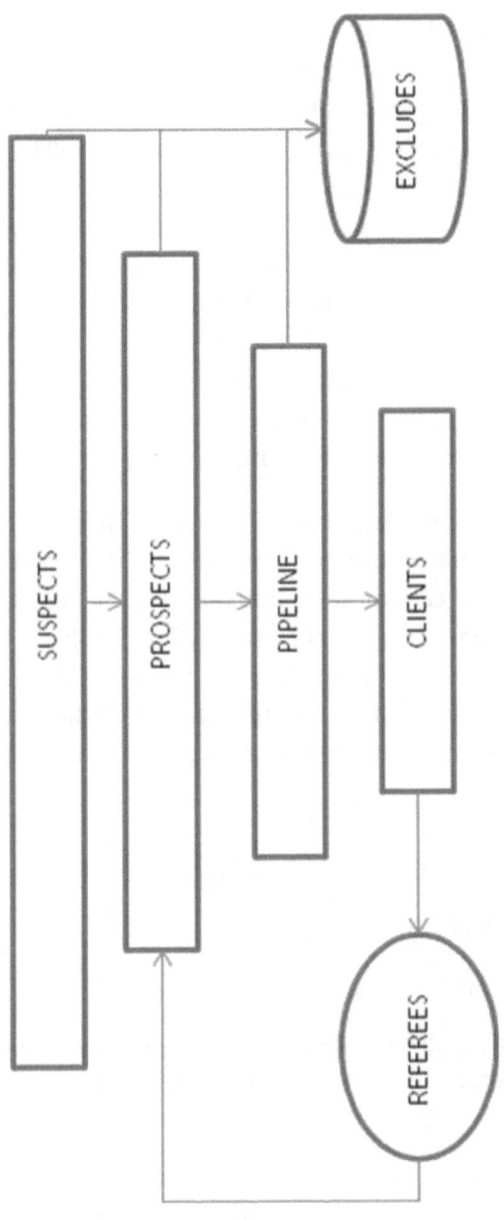

6.1   Data Capture

Gathering as much information as possible about a customer is hugely beneficial. The more contact information you have about a customer the easier they will be to get in touch with, the more you know about their company, the easier it will be to build rapport and the more you know about their situation, the more able you will be able to find a solution for that customer that is suitable to them, which is competitive enough to win the business for you. Don't rely on memory for all this information. Customise your database to gather each piece of information, both contact data and other vital data capture.

As alluded to earlier, on each call you should be looking to capture more and more information about each contact, even if you cannot take the call very far, always try to achieve something on that call by looking for a blank on your database and trying to get it filled in. On the first call you are mainly looking to improve your contact data, even if you are not speaking with the decision maker directly:

- Decision maker's name

- Decision maker's position

- Direct phone number

- Email address

- Establish their requirement (do they a need for that service at all i.e. do they meet your customer profile)

On subsequent calls you will be looking for more and more specific information and keeping notes on who you have spoken to and what has been discussed. Things you would try and capture for each contact might include:

- Current suppliers

- Current spend

- Current concerns

- Due dates

- Average order size/demand levels

- Frequency of requirements

- Procurement process

- Likely duration of contract

- Budget available

The more of this information you can capture, the more likely you are to secure a sale. If you can make your products/services meet your client's requirements you have an excellent chance at getting a sale. This means you have to ask the right questions (more on this later) and get excellent levels of detail from your customer. On your first call it is important that you bear in mind all the information that will be of benefit to you. It is likely that you will have a database with space for this type of information. If you think that there is a useful piece of information that is missing from your database, for instance, it does have a space for the date that the client will next review that product/service, add it, or speak to your line manager.

6.2   Notes

Keeping notes is of vital importance. Keeping notes differs from data capture in that your data capture should be aiming to get the same information about each company and your notes should be unique to each company. Just like previously discussed, when you're speaking to different people or people are on holiday, here's a quick example of why notes can be very useful:

'spoke to Susan – advised I should send information to Geoff via email (geoff@carworld.com) as he is on holiday in Spain at the moment – call back in 2 weeks'.

The email address here would also go in the relevant database slot, along with Geoff's surname and direct dial phone number.

Your notes can help you maintain and build rapport further. You can pick up where you left off and also use it to keep your call warm and unique to each company. For instance, here you may never have spoken to Geoff and when you come to call back two weeks later, won't specifically recall the conversation with Susan, as it may have been quite brief. However, you can ask to speak to Geoff and when you get through to Geoff ask if he had a nice time in Spain and name drop Susan as being the person who recommended that you send through the details. Already you are much further ahead that simply opening with 'I sent you some of our details', which is much colder.

This is also applicable to your approach as a customer focused sales person. Here's an example:

Claire sells recruitment services and is in contact with a large wholesaler. Someone she speaks mentions that she needs to speak to Steve, the Warehouse Manager as they are getting busy in the warehouse and might be looking for more people to help pack deliveries and load vans but Steve is currently not available and advises that Claire should call back later. She could make specific notes about this, which will feed into her next call or simply call back and make a run of the mill call.

Would you rather be the agency who followed up with, 'Hi Steve, are you looking to recruit any more members of staff as yet?' or 'Good afternoon Steve, it's Claire from All One Recruitment, still busy in the warehouse?' The one with the best notes, will recall their customer's needs a lot more accurately. In essence the two callers are doing the same thing, however, Claire is paying attention to the company that she is speaking to and these slight changes in her language from generic to specific will make her stand out as professional. However, she would not be able to be so professional on a consistent basis without keeping good notes to remind herself of the specifics of each conversation.

I could give many examples of this of course but I will simply emphasise that you keep detailed notes as use them to build the relationship as you go from call to call. Things that you should be looking to keep notes on include:

- Each person you have spoken to

- Any rapport that you have built

- Any personal details attained (that can be used for rapport – nothing too personal!)

- Any objections

- Any specific requirements

- Previous experiences (e.g. with other suppliers)

- Anything else you need to remember on the next call!

6.3   Inbound data capture

On an inbound line, sales may not be your only activity and so grouping customers in this way may not be possible. You may only take calls from existing customers (i.e. everyone's already a 'client') and you might just be looking to up-sell new or additional services to them.

However, in a way you can keep a list of 'prospects' of your own by keeping a list of those worth following up with in the near future in some way, shape or form and think about highlighting sales opportunities and buying signals (chapter 13) in your notes so that if you or a colleague get another opportunity to speak to the customer again, a good opportunity is not lost.

Always take the opportunity to fill in the blanks on the customer's contact details too. You might not see the benefit of this directly but that data capture improves both sales and customer services:

1) If you were to take an email address from a customer that wasn't previously there, they might respond to an email shot and purchase a new product or service that they otherwise wouldn't have, and;

2) Whilst taking the details you could begin a new line of conversation that leads to a sale as you continue to build rapport and learn more about the customer.

Section B
<u>The Follow Up Call</u>

Section B – The Follow Up Call

The follow up call tends to be where you get into the real 'nitty gritty' of being a sales person on the phone. It's where you are speaking to the stronger prospects in your database, where you gather a lot more information and make your full pitch. Don't make the mistake of thinking that this is where the sale begins because as we've seen, your introduction influences your customer and is truly where the sale begins.

In an ideal world you can get through to your decision maker and build enough rapport to get through a lot of this information in one call. There is nothing to stop you moving onto these steps all in call one but more often than not you will have to break up calls due to people's availability and wanting to look over information before continuing discussing your product/service.

Let's look at what you need to achieve from this stage of the call. First we need to be sure that we've covered the basics as laid out in Section A. At this stage of the call the customer should be a 'prospect'. Referring back to the groups discussed earlier a prospect should fit into the following situation:

- Full name of the decision maker

- Thorough contact details – address, phone number and email address (as many of these as possible)

- Fit customer profile, company size, location, sector etc

Tony Pearson

- Have expressed an interest in your services (i.e. requested further information or asked for call back)

- Introductory information has been sent

At this stage you are speaking to the decision maker (or member of the decision making team), you have fully qualified all your contact data and have direct contact details for the decision maker, identified that the company fit into your recognised customer profile, have some level of requirement for your services in the not too distant future and have been introduced to your company both verbally and with introductory literature. This is an ideal prospect, I appreciate that the odd element of this may still be missing before you proceed. If you are missing any of the above, just ensure that you cover it as soon as you get the opportunity during your follow up call.

Your 'follow up call' may end up being several calls depending on the immediacy of your customer's need, the size of the purchase that you are discussing and their availability for discussions over the phone and meetings that you are looking to arrange. It is very rare that a company is able to make a buying decision after such a small amount of contact with a new company.

Section C deals with closing business, which comes after you have had the time to present your company and discuss the customer's requirements in detail by which time they are a much stronger prospect to buy your services. There are no specific guidelines for where each call will begin and end so do not feel that I am encouraging you to qualify a customer as a prospect, put the phone down and call them a week later to follow up, get an excellent level of interest from them, put the phone down and call back a week later to close the deal. You know as well as I do that calls will ebb and flow as naturally as they like. This entire book can be achieved in one call or it could take months on end and dozens of calls before you get the result, mainly depending on your customer's position. Therefore I make no specific point about when to hang up the phone and when to follow up etc, but do encourage driving the call(s) forward by professionally achieving all the information, rapport and quality sales presentation you possibly can, however long this make take.

7.0 Establishing the Customers Needs

The most important aspect of any sale of any product or service is right here in establishing your customer's needs/requirements. Yes there's plenty of work to do to get here but nothing is more key to securing business that really getting to know your customer and how your product/service fits with them and their business.

You do this by asking your customer lots of good questions about them and how they might use your product/service and matching what they say to what you do. In the next few sections we are going to look at questioning techniques, rapport building and meeting these requirements.

First, I want to give you an example of the effects of establishing the customer's needs before making a sales pitch. This is an example that we will come back to as we develop these ideas:

Imagine walking into a car showroom or forecourt that sells a large range of new and used cars. You are on your own. You are greeted by a smiling man in a suit. He looks pleasant enough but you know nothing more about him. He however, knows something about you. In this situation you are already a prospect because in retail sales, you use advertising to get to your suspects and those who walk through the door are already prospects. (i.e. why else would they come into your shop/equivalent if they weren't at least partly interested in what you sell?). He therefore doesn't really need to worry about introducing who the company are or what they do at this stage. This is his 'follow up call'.

You are stood looking at a sparkling new car just outside the showroom. The smiling man speaks, 'Ah, the new Audi A4. Very good looking car. It has an excellent engine, two litres, diesel, injection. Good economy, it'll probably do thirty to the gallon round town and fifty to the gallon on the motorway. ABS breaks, CD Player with a four CD changer. Plenty of room in the back if you have kids and a large boot for shopping and what not. Fancy a test drive?'

What are your thoughts? How do you feel about the salesman? He hasn't been rude and he's shown a good knowledge about the car you happened to be looking at. He's offering for you to drive the car, in a 'no obligation' kind of way. But what has he missed? He's missed a lot but to sum it up, he's missed 'the point'! This is the same sales pitch that he would give to every customer who walked through the door (or walked onto the forecourt).

Now imagine being stood by the same car. The same smiling man comes over and this time asks how you are and then says to you, 'Good morning. Tell me about your ideal car...'.

How do you now feel? Like he's taking an interest in you? Far less pressured? Like if you buy something today, it's going to be *exactly* what you're looking for? And you've not even answered his question yet! The power of questions is extraordinary and we're going to look at those in more detail in the next chapter. This is just one example of how you can look at the sales process entirely from the customer's point of view. If you were the customer what would you want to happen? What type of people do you buy from? What makes you *want* to buy? What type of person would you be happy referring friends, family and colleagues to? We'll also be coming back to the smiling car salesman.

If you approach each sales call with the mentality that you are going to establish the customer's requirements before you sell them anything you will be a far, far more successful sales person. This means being willing to understand that not everyone wants or can benefit from your product and service and using techniques to open up your customer and finding ways in which they can benefit.

7.1   Inbound – assessing customer needs

As an inbound sales person, this is the part of sales that gives you a major advantage over an outbound sales team and should provide excellent sales opportunities call after call.

If a customer has called through with a general enquiry or problem that you are able to help with, you would have opened a dialogue where the customer is feeling relaxed and providing you with lots of good information about their situation. You most likely also have their account details or equivalent available in front of you when they call (assuming that they are an existing customer that is). Your first and foremost mission is of course to solve that customer's query or issue but throughout the call you can be looking for sales opportunities. Things that they mention, which link to things that you can offer them.

Providing you have handled their call satisfactorily, you have the opportunity to revisit something they mentioned and begin to question them further. The very issue/ enquiry they called you with will expose much about their circumstances, giving you plenty of time to align anything you sell to meet their needs.

8.0 Questions

If you already do telesales/lead generation (or have done in the past), take a moment to think about how you have used questions in your sales. Do you feel that you ask enough questions? What type of questions did you ask? What were the benefits?

A lot of sales training focuses around open and closed questions. Open questions being 'who, what, where, when, why and how' questions and closed questions being those that can be answered with a 'yes/no'. This is somewhat inaccurate and not exactly useful. The 'who, what, where, when, why and how' questions are not in fact the most open questions you can use. They actual tend to ask for specific pieces of information rather than help you build the whole picture. The techniques described below are actually used in journalism but work brilliantly in sales. Read through the rest of the chapter and bear it in mind the next time you read an interview in a magazine/newspaper or hear a television/radio interview. The 'interviewee' is much like our customer. The interviewer or sales person needs to extract information from the subject, get them comfortable, get them talking and guide them in a particular direction. They also need to not be the one doing most of the talking!

As an overview, you should start with open questions to really get the customer talking, about themselves, the subject you have presented as well as their likes and dislikes about the matter. Use fact-finding questions to fill in any gaps of information you need or extract more detail in particular areas and used closing questions to call them to action, i.e. close the sale.

8.1   Open Questions

A lot of sales trainers mistake fact-finding questions as described below to be open-ended questions. They are not in fact the most open questions you can ask.

Open questions are those which your customer can answer with as much detail as possible. Open questions begin with words such as, 'Tell me...', 'Describe...' and 'Explain...'. Here are some examples:

'Tell me about your previous experience in this sector...'

'Explain your plans for business growth to me...'

'Talk me through your buying procedures...'

'Describe your ideal package...'

Remember the smiling car salesman from earlier? What question did he ask to get you excited and get you talking? 'Tell me about your ideal car...' You could talk and talk about all the things you love and hate about cars, talk about exactly what you're looking for and why, without the salesman asking another question so this is how effective this type of questioning can be. Of course, your customers aren't always going to just talk and talk and give you all the information you need one question one but at least you would have opened them up. You can then look to fill in the gaps by asking fact finding questions (see below).

It you're a stickler for grammar and have noticed that these open questions don't have question marks and cannot therefore technically be questions don't worry. I am aware that grammatically they are not questions but in practice they are excellent for getting information from your customers because they are questions worded as instructions so you are far more likely to get a detailed response.

N.B. If you are asking an open question do not use any of the following during that sentence, 'who, what, where, when, why, how'. For instance, 'Tell me what your ideal car is...'. First, it sounds even more like an instruction and second you're actually asking a fact-finding question and not an open one. i.e. the 'Tell me' in this example doesn't serve a purpose, other than making you sound bossy! Look again at the examples above and notice the complete absence of 'who, what, where, when, why and how'.

The more a person talks to you about themselves (or their business) the more they begin to trust you and appreciate that you are taking an interest. People rarely tire of talking about themselves! The more information you have the easier it is to match up your product/service to their situation, i.e. meet their requirement (see below) and the more opportunities there are to build rapport.

The smiling car salesman has just asked you to tell him about your ideal car. Of course unless you are very fortunate, your 'ideal' car isn't what you're actually looking to purchase that day but it's still a great opener. The salesman could even be slightly more practical and ask, 'Tell me about the car you're looking for...'.

I can't speak for you specifically but here's an example answer:

'I would love a large Mercedes but it's a bit out of my price range unfortunately! I'm probably looking for a medium size car, definitely five doors, that's economical to run both on fuel and insurance. Two to three years old without already having done too many miles. I'll mainly be using it for business, up and down motorways so was probably thinking about a Volkswagen or a Ford'.

How many 'whos', 'whats', 'wheres', 'whens', 'whys' and 'hows' would it have taken to get this list of information? Definitely more than one. Try and think of a positive open question to bring in near the beginning of speaking to a prospect to get them talking about their situation as a whole. You can then save all the 'w's and the 'h' for the next part of your questioning.

8.2   Fact-finding Questions

So, we've already ticked a few boxes with one question. We've answered 'how new/old would you like the car to be?', 'how large a car?', 'how important is fuel consumption?', 'what manufacturer preferences do you have?', 'what will you mainly be using the car for?', without making it sound like twenty questions. You now have two great opportunities: 1) to ask some rapport building questions based on what you've just heard, and 2) ask some fact finding questions to further understand what car your customer is likely to go for.

So, what other information might be useful at this point? The salesman could ask the following:

What colours do you prefer? What models have you seen that interest you? How much were you looking to spend? i.e. fill in the gaps until you have enough information to provide a solution to your customer, developing rapport along the way.

Fact-finding questions are fantastic for extracting specific information. Ensure that after the initial open questions you use these questions to keep your customer talking and guide them in a specific direction. Make sure that you are not asking closed questions (those that can be answered with a 'yes/no').

In your database you should have some key data capture entries that are required. For instance, size of company, current suppliers, etc. Fact-finding questions are ideal to get these boxes filled in, if the details haven't already come up in conversation. Remember to get round to these questions as naturally as possible in order to prevent yourself from sounding scripted. If your customer is talking don't rush them to answer certain questions, wait for a lull in the conversation before changing subject. You should be very pleased when a customer is talking openly as you will be building rapport (see next chapter) and be in no rush to interrupt them.

Here are some generic examples of fact-finding questions that you could adapt to use in your calling:

What factors are most important to you?

Who have you used previously for these services (i.e. current supplier)?

How are you looking to develop your business in this area?

When are you next due to review your current supplier?

8.3   Closing Questions

Again there is a very common misconception that a 'closed' question is a question that can only be answered with either a 'yes' or 'no'. This is not entirely accurate and I don't mean that someone could also answer these questions with a 'maybe'!

A much better definition of a 'closed' question is a question which presents a limited number of options. It just so happens that the two options that are most commonly presented with this type of question are 'yes' and 'no'. Examples of a closed question where the answers aren't going to be a 'yes' or 'no' is, 'do you prefer apples or bananas?', 'are you right or left handed?' and 'does my hair look better long or short?'.

Notice that this section is called 'closing' questions and not 'closed' questions. That is because, even though you may ask a question that only elicits a 'yes/no' answer, you can use them to serve a purpose. You can use them to close the conversation at the right moment and call your customer to action. Here are some great examples:

Is that what you're looking for?

Are you happy with that?

Can we get you signed up now?

Would you like me to do that for you?

Can I take your order?

Of course, these questions can be answered with a 'no'. In which case you might have to back track to readdress some of your customer's issues or you might simply be dealing with someone who isn't that interested in buying.

However, a 'yes' here is a sale. No 'umming' and 'arring' or waiting for them to ask you if they can buy it. Ask! If it's a 'no', find out why, if it's a 'yes' you have a sale – do the paperwork!

You will notice, going through this guide, that the sales approach is pretty relaxed. We spend a lot of time talking about the niceties of sales but there is one pitfall to taking a more laid back approach to sales and that is worrying solely about getting along with your customer and not closing the deal. The general overall idea is to help your customer find what they want and to build a good relationship in order to maximise the opportunities though there will always come a point when you will need to call your customer to action and seal the deal.

When it comes to closing the deal your customer will appreciate that you have acted swiftly and efficiently in order to deal with their request. Keep the customer service/ customer focused element of your job going throughout completing the deal and remember that one yes is sufficient. You don't need to keep asking the customer – they might get tired of you asking and change their mind!

We will look at closing techniques in more detail later, though it is in closing the deal that closed/closing questions are particularly useful. In section C I will be providing you with some specific closing techniques but we're not at that stage quite yet. This is where we will look more at closing questions that don't simply present a 'yes' or 'no' option.

8.4   Questioning techniques flow chart

<u>Open Questions</u>

(Tell me, describe, explain, talk me through)

Examples:

- Tell me more about your future plans...

- Describe your average order...

- Talk me through the problems you've experienced previously...

<u>Fact-finding Questions</u>

(who, what, where, when, why, how)

Examples:

- Who would be best to speak to?

- What is the most important aspect of this for you?

- Who have you used previously?

- When are you next due to review your providers?

- How do you think this would fit into your current situation?

Closing Questions

(Can, Do, Shall, Would, Is etc)

Examples:

- Does that sound good to you?

- Would you like me to do that for you?

- Shall we make that order for you?

- Is there anything else that you need to know before we proceed?

- Do you prefer option A or option B?

You may wish to make a similar list of questions that are relevant to what you sell and keep this close to hand.

9.0 Rapport

Every sales person who works in sales claims to build an excellent rapport with their clients. Rapport is key to biding you enough time on the telephone to get through all the details you need to in order to achieve a sale. But what exactly is rapport?

A lot of people who work in sales simply think that rapport is being able to have a chit-chat whilst also talking about business, unfortunately, this is inaccurate. Rapport isn't something you do, it's a level you achieve with your client. Rapport is dictionary defined as 'a relation or connection, especially a harmonious or sympathetic relation'. It has more in common with words such as 'fellowship', 'camaraderie' and 'understanding', than it does, 'nattering', 'casual conversation' or 'exchanging pleasantries', to give you some idea.

If we take a leap forward, rapport is something you have with existing clients. They know you and what you do, you know them and what they do and you've spoken on dozens of occasions about a whole manner of things. You have a business relationship. You have achieved rapport with this client.

How do we then achieve rapport with more customers? There are many factors that help to build rapport over your initial calls. You are building rapport throughout every step of the call because you do not only build rapport when you are chatting about something that isn't something to do with business. You build rapport when your customer finds you interesting (a good introduction – chapter 1), when you are polite and professional (chapter 2), when you get to know more about your client's business (asking questions – chapter 7), when you make what you are selling appropriate to them (meeting customer needs - chapter 11) and when you can talk on their level about things that they find important (product knowledge – chapter 9). Rapport is gradual but if you go about your entire call in the right way, can be achieved at a heightened pace.

As earlier discussed, you apply these principles to whoever you are speaking to at the company, regardless of whether or not they are the decision maker as a good level of rapport with a colleague can be carried over when you start speaking to the decision maker. The phone is passed over with a smile, they are more trusting of you and you possibly have a lot more to talk about that you would have done otherwise.

Rapport is built through confidence, professionalism, good product knowledge, being deemed trustworthy, being interesting, being friendly etc etc etc. Here are a few 'non-business' areas that can assist with overall rapport building.

9.1   Safe Bets

You may think that the weather is a good way to build rapport but it simply isn't interesting. (Unless there has been a ridiculous amount of snow /large storm/heat wave in the last 24 hours). There are other good areas to build rapport in.

The easiest thing to do is look for something that the customer brings up. If they mention sport, talk about sport, if they mention the weather, talk about the weather but always ensure that you are on safe ground in terms of (1) talking about something you know about, and (2) not saying something that could offend/upset anyone.

If someone mentions that they played golf over the weekend and you don't know anything about golf, simply ask them if they enjoyed it, if they do it most weekends etc. Don't try and talk about the Ryder Cup because you'll just sound a bit dim and may come across as a bit of a suck-up. Just as you would get caught out talking about products and services that you aren't knowledgeable about, the same goes for non-business matters.

9.2 Unsafe areas

Never swear. Not even words that are a bit close to the cuff so to speak. If someone doesn't know you very well and your language is a bit too course, it can be very off putting.

Politics. Definitely an area to be avoided. Discussing personal politics is far too risky a business. Particularly if a customer raises an idea that you don't entirely agree with. Never enter into a debate with a customer. If they do begin talking about a subject that you disagree with or at least disagree with their point of view, simply change the subject and try and bring the conversation back round to business. Rapport cannot be built up in a heated debate!

Your weekend plans. Sometimes it's quite nice to ask the customer what their evening or weekend plans are, particularly if you're speaking to them on a Friday for instance. However, regardless of what the customer says they're up to, try to keep the conversation about them and not about you. If they ask by all means answer but try and maintain the professionalism that you've spent so long building up. Declaring that you're going to spend your whole weekend drinking with your friends will somewhat undermine all that hard work!

9.3 Current Events

It's amazing how something as simple as reading a newspaper in the morning can help with your sales! Of course, this goes for Internet news too. If you spent ten-fifteen minutes at the beginning of the day reading the headline stories that day and any areas that were applicable to your business you have given yourself rapport fodder right there.

If someone mentions a major news story and you haven't got a clue what they're talking about, it might make you seem somewhat ignorant. If they mention something you can get into a conversation about, it builds rapport.

The business news is of course very important, especially anything relating to your sector. At the time of writing we are in the midst of a recession, which affects practically every business in the country. It's the topic on most people's lips and being able to communicate with customers on an informed level about this subject is helping build rapport with new clients experiencing the effect's of the economic downturn. Once again, political opinions should be avoided.

9.4   Geography

You might not have liked geography at school but it's something very useful for your sales! Especially, if your job revolves around speaking to, booking appointments with or delivering goods and services to people nationwide. Knowing what places are close by, how far away they are from you, how long it would take to get there, what county a town is in, can all make you sound more intelligent and make you more familiar with your client as you are able to discuss something that you both have knowledge of.

Keeping a map on the wall or a road atlas by your desk is a fantastic tool to help get appointments booked. Imagine the impact of statements such as, 'you're only about an hour away from us so it would be very easy for us to call in for a chat at your convenience' and 'you're just a few junctions down the M1 from us so a meeting would be very easy for us to do'. It's yet another way of tailoring the call to be more specific to each customer you speak to, rather than going for the same pitch to each person. Again, this is not chatting about something that is irrelevant in order to build rapport, it is further establishing the connection between you and your customer.

Your geographical knowledge can also help you win business from competitors. Imagine you were a stationery company who delivered to clients nationwide. You are based in Leicester and you contact a company based in Nottingham. Their current provider is based in Newcastle. Now it doesn't take much of a geography expert to know that Leicester is a lot closer to Nottingham than Newcastle is but unless you bring up the subject you cannot build rapport around it and highlight the benefits of having a more local provider (more in chapter 10).

9.5   Key interest

Try to find a subject, which really engages the customer's interest. I have to be honest and say that I have a lot of customer's that I talk to football about for an example. This is ideal for any of your customers who are interested in football because each time you call them something new would have happened that you can bring up to get them talking about something topical and interesting to them, building rapport. As you can probably tell, I'm a football fan but if my customer isn't interested in it then neither am I. At least not during that conversation, why would I want to bring up a subject that my customer has no interest in?

Boring your customer or dominating the conversation is not a good way to build rapport.

The subject that you're looking for with each client is something that you can bring up in as many calls as possible so sports and other hobbies as well as business news and other current events are ideal. This is the reason that people bring up the weather, it's topical and something that both parties can relate to but it's also unfortunately, incredibly dull. You won't stand out from the crowd by being the person who mentions the rain or sun every time you call, you will only achieve this by finding a key interest for each particular customer and engaging with them in this. The customer will then feel that they have found someone who they can relate to rather than another run of the mill cold caller. This is particularly effective when it something specific to them, their kids, their hobbies, their football team, their favourite television show etc.

Remember, regardless of how long the conversation is and how you feel that you will remember this the next time you speak to them, you're likely to have a lot of conversations in between so make good notes! You don't want to kick yourself for not doing and missing a good and quite obvious opportunity.

9.6   Active listening

It is important that whilst you are listening to your customer answer all the questions that you are asking of them that you acknowledge what is being said with relevant verbal indicators such as, 'really', 'I see', 'that's interesting' etc. This may be something you do quite naturally but making yourself consciously aware of it can help you to use your acknowledgements more effectively.

Making these acknowledgements has two main effects. One, it shows that you are paying close attention to what your customer is saying, backing up the impression that your aim is to help them as an individual customer, rather than simply going through a routine before trying to sell the same thing in the same way over and over again. And two, it will encourage them to speak for longer. Conversation involves natural turn-taking where once someone has been speaking for a while without interruption they will naturally stop and allow the other person to speak. If you have been gently expressing an interest in what they have been saying throughout the time that they were speaking, they will naturally speak for longer as they are less likely to feel as if they are dominating the conversation, something you want them to do in order to build further rapport.

However, this can work against you if you say too much. Only use very short acknowledgements as not to interrupt the customer's flow. If you talk for longer you may guide them away from what they were saying or make them feel as if you've heard enough. If they are talking about something that reminds you of existing or previous clients, make a note of it for a later conversation. You can use it as an example of how you helped someone in a similar situation, if you interrupt them to say, 'yes, we have a customer who was in the same position as you...' it may sound as if you have heard enough and categorised them, which is not treating them as an individual. Coming back to these points can also be very effective. A phrase such as, 'you mentioned early that you have experienced problems with your deliveries, tell me more about that...' shows that you were paying close attention and gives you the opportunity to guide the customer further down a route that could help you highlight some advantages of your company. You are actively engaged with the customer at this point, simply by giving them the room to speak freely and taking an active interest.

You need to ensure that your acknowledgements are well varied. If you keep using the same one your customer will notice this and it will distract them. When you do this by habit it is known as a 'weasel word' that just keeps sneaking into your speech without you noticing (see chapter 8.8).

9.7   Positive Language

The power of positive language is quite astounding. This is a tool you can use to subconsciously win your customer over. Particularly useful for selling over the phone as so much more rides on *what* you say because of the absence of body language etc.

By acknowledging what your customer says or by beginning a lot of your sentences with superlatives you can influence your customer into a positive mental state. 'Great', 'super', 'lovely', 'wonderful', 'fantastic', 'that's really good', 'smashing', 'perfect', 'ideal' and so on. Just reading those few words has probably perked you up a small amount. The more you can use these words during your call, the more your customer will be endeared towards you and feel more comfortable dealing with you, an excellent rapport building technique. It all adds to the good feeling they get when they speak to you. Quite often sales people can get confrontational on the phone with a customer, as soon as this happens, rapport is dissolved and a deal of any kind is very unlikely.

These positive utterances can be used even to lift the most mundane parts of the call. If someone was a bit too busy to speak to you, they might ask you to call back later, to which rather than simply saying, 'okay, I'll try again later', you can say, 'that's perfect, I'll give you a call this afternoon, I look forward to speaking to you then'. If you say this with genuine positive tone of voice, it doesn't sound cheesy, it sounds positive, patient, polite and professional. All the 'P's we're looking for!

One very effective way that I have seen this used is when someone mentions a competitor at an early stage in the call. Perhaps before you've qualified them as a prospect. Rather than just saying, 'oh, okay, do you mind if I send you some of our literature for your files and perhaps call back in six months' (which would keep them as a suspect in your database) positive language can steer the declaration of a rival company to be a stepping stone in the conversation rather than a barrier. Instead, a phrase such as, 'that's great, they're a good company. However, we've many client's who've found that they can get a better service at an even better rate with ourselves so would you like to look over some of our literature?' You can take further details, upgrade them to a prospect and follow up as the call is still warm.

Try and replace words in your call such as, 'sure', 'no problem', 'alright' and 'okay' with more uplifting words. These words are acceptable acknowledgements but aren't exactly going to brighten up your customer's day. Being prepared for the negative from the customer can help you reply with good, positive language. Never be surprised that the customer isn't jumping for joy at receiving your call but don't reduce yourself to feeling like a burden to them, remain positive and they are much more likely to perk up and follow your lead.

9.8   Weasel Words

Here's a tricky bit of telesales to get right and it's something that pretty much everyone will do. Weasel words are those empty, filling words that we use to pad out what we're saying, even though they are absolutely meaningless to the sentence that we are trying to convey. They also tend to be idiosyncrasies, which are very difficult for you to pick up on as you do these things naturally. The easiest way to pick these up is to record your calls, which your company may well do or ask a colleague who has heard you make a lot of calls. What you are looking for are those words that you repeat far too many times during a call and usually don't serve a purpose. Examples include, 'no problem' – there was probably never going to have been a problem, 'obviously' – if it's actually obvious you don't need to say the sentence at all, 'okay', 'of course', 'bear with me' and so on. These words do naturally creep into conversation but if you can iron them out and be more concise with how you speak to your customer, they will have more respect for what you are telling them as you will sound more confident about what you are selling. It is important to keep a good variety of acknowledgements and superlatives otherwise they begin to have to opposite effect and your client picks up on the fact that you always say a particular word. With a good variety of positive, concise language you will quickly build up more interest from your customer.

Customer Focused Sales – checkpoint 2.

By this stage we have spent a lot of time looking at the customer. Who they are, what they do, why they might buy from you etc. We're now going to look at the different areas where we can start to meet those customer needs. A customer could tell you their life story but unless you make what you are selling relevant to them and make your pitch all you have had is a nice chat and no sale!

This is your sales presentation. Brought in when we've learnt all that we can about the customer. Think for a moment once again from the customer's point of view. You've managed to open the customer up to talk about their situation and build some good rapport but the customer is under no disillusion that there is a sale of some sort yet to come. The impact of this is far softer when it really is tailored to suit the person you've been speaking to.

Here's how to begin presenting your company and all the things you need to consider along with this.

10.0 Product Knowledge

Product knowledge is arguably fifty percent of what is needed for sales. The other fifty percent being good sales and people skills, which is covered in all the other sections of this book. You can be the best sales person in the world but unless you know the ins and outs of what you are selling you will sell diddley-squat (to give it it's technical term).

If you are selling cars, you need to know about cars, if you are selling holidays, you need to know about your destinations, if you are selling recruitment services you need to know about the recruitment process and vetting personnel etc. I know this sounds like stating the obvious but ask yourself this, could I know more about what I/we do? Could I know more about the marketplace? Could I know more about what our competitors offer? And so on. The more knowledgeable you are the more you will sell (with a reasonable amount of people skills of course).

I have trained people before who've worked with their company for a number of years and were unable to tell me who the main competitors were, what accreditations the company had and what the significance of those were, couldn't give me a ball park figure for an example quote. Scary, I know, but true nonetheless.

10.1 Product knowledge
Knowledge about your products and services is key. The more you know about your stock/company/service the easier you can control a call through prompt and confident answers. Having to go away to check on something for a customer has two negative effects. One it shows you to be a person who is looking to sell first and other concerns come later (i.e. you have very poor product knowledge) and it also delays a conversation that might have been going quite well, turning it cold. Would you buy from someone who you felt didn't know what they were talking about regardless of how pleasant or professional they were?

If a customer asked for an example price for something this is a strong buying signal (we will come back to buying signals later). For instance, if you are selling recruitment services and someone asks you this question, 'most of our new starters have a basic salary of £15,000, how much would it cost to recruit someone at that level?'. This is quite obviously a buying signal and if you reply promptly and confidently with an answer such as, 'we would charge 15% of that salary, which would work out to £2,250 per candidate. If you were looking at recruiting several people at once we could look to offer you a slightly better rate than that as well'. This will maintain the customer's interest even if they wish to try and negotiate straight away. They are still 'warm' and interested. If the response to the same question was, 'erm, I'll just check on that for you...' and the customer was placed on hold, they wouldn't be all that impressed and their interest would wane. Why would they want to buy from someone who doesn't know precisely how they can help?! You're possibly thinking, 'why would anyone make a sales call without knowing such basics?' but you'd be surprised! The principle is the same for the more complex aspects of what you sell. Though I'm pretty sure the vast majority of recruitment telesales personnel do know their prices perfectly, it's an example.

The more you know your products, the more information you can give to your client which will potentially help you meet their requirements (chapter 11) and you could also give multiple options which will help you close the deal (chapter 17.1). Good product knowledge can also help you build rapport (chapter 8) especially when you are speaking about any specialist or technical service. From this you can see how important excellent product knowledge can be.

I'm sure you know your products well but a great question to ask yourself on a regular basis is, 'how could I know more about what I sell?'.

If sales is 50% product knowledge it is possible that I should have talked about product knowledge right at the beginning of this book, screaming, 'make sure you know your onions before even bothering to read on!'. However, we are walking through a call in order and it is not until this sort of stage that you should be looking to display your product knowledge any further than a basic introduction as to what your company does. (Recall the smiling car salesman's first approach, lots of product knowledge but no interest in the customer as an individual.) You should have taken the time to establish what the customer is looking for and then begin to show your product knowledge.

10.2 Sector knowledge

Knowing your company's brochure, client list, price list etc is unfortunately not sufficient. You must also know about the wider sector that both you and your customer work in. You and your customer are not necessarily in the same sector. You might be selling telecoms services into the manufacturing sector or recruitment services into the financial sector, however, knowing both of these sectors well is very important. Current events/trends, the biggest companies in the sector, industry bodies, standard accreditations etc.

We're now well past the stage of your call where you have understood a bit about your client's business and hopefully a fair bit about how they currently source your services, who they use at present etc (I'll speak more about competitors shortly). You should be well up on how your sector operates and what alternatives are available to the customer. If you are a wholesaler in a particular sector you should know what the typical minimum orders are, what prices are like, what terms and conditions are usually available to customers (can they get sale of return? can they get 60 day billing allowances?) on so on and so forth.

To further help your rapport and appear knowledgeable, try and read publications and websites relating to your client's sector. Being the one company who is aware of upcoming changes in legislation, current problems in the sector and new innovations in the sector will really make you stand out and encourage the customer to be thinking that you're the company to be dealing with.

Remember, this is not a trick to dupe the customer into thinking you know what you're talking about. Reading these kinds of materials is research which will support your ability to provide a quality service to your customers. You may even have to do such research on your own time as not to reduce the time you can spend on the phone, which might be an abhorrent idea to some but if you're reading books such as this there is obviously a desire to improve and wider reading surrounding your target market will help you achieve this. Discuss with your line manager to see if there are any quiet times during the week that you can dedicate to research.

10.3 Competitors

Knowing your main competitors is a huge advantage to you when the customer mentions who their current supplier/ provider is. If you know that you are cheaper than a company, you can tell the customer, if you know that you offer a wider range of services, you can tell the customer, if you are located closer to the customer you can tell them that the relationship would be easier to manage and so on and so forth.

Never bad mouth your competitors. Never. The examples above simply highlight the potential advantages of using your company. If you say that another company are rubbish in any way, this will only reflect badly on you. Your customer could have a good relationship with their supplier and you bad mouthing someone they already use will get you nowhere. You will also be using negative language, which subconsciously turns the customer away from you.

Here's an example of what you could say when a competitor's name is mentioned, 'I know ABC Motors, they're very good, though a lot of our customers like our 30 day money back guarantee, which is something that I don't think ABC motors offer'. You are then adding value to a service that they already pay for. I'm sure you can see the impact a sentence like this could have. You are subliminally saying, 'we can offer you everything you already have plus more!' without sounding cheesy or vague. This will always capture your customer's attention and you do not sound nasty, unprofessional or desperate.

Performing a SWOT (Strengths, Weaknesses, Opportunities, Threats) analysis on your main five competitors will have you well prepared for handling the objection of the customer mentioning a current provider as you will be ready with the relevant benefit to hand. This is likely something that your company has already done during their market research and latest sales and marketing strategy, though being fully clued in on this will aid your calling significantly. More on what to include in a SWOT is covered in the next chapter.

11.0 USP's, Features & Benefits

You should always have a list of Unique Selling Points (USPs), features and benefits to hand when making a sales call. I'll distinguish between each one shortly for you. The mistake a lot of telesales people make is to reel off these selling points at first given opportunity rather than do all the leg work we've already been through before using them. If you simply say all your selling points back-to-back they lose their impact because they just merge together and might not be applicable to that particular customer.

I like to think of it as a shooting game. Sad, I know, but helpful. What I mean is that I wait for the customer to put up a target, whether it's an objection or a mention of what they currently do and I shoot it with a USP, feature or benefit. Maybe it's more like tennis. Maybe I should stop making rubbish metaphors and get back to the point! The point is that your selling points will have far more impact if used at the appropriate moment during your call.

We've already seen one example of this above when adding value to their current situation when the customer mentioned a competitor that they used. We added a feature. A '30 day money-back guarantee' that our competitor did not offer. We waited until our customer mentioned something about their situation and we matched one of our selling points to it. You will only elicit this kind of information from your customers by asking good questions.

Our smiling car salesman from earlier gave a perfect example for this earlier. He reeled off a long list of selling points before he'd established exactly what we were looking for. Simple selling features can sound a lot more tempting when introduced correctly. For instance look at the list of selling points the salesman reeled off in our example: 'Ah, the new Audi A4. Very good looking car. It has an excellent engine, two litres, diesel, injection. Good economy, it'll probably do thirty to the gallon round town and fifty to the gallon on the motorway. ABS breaks, CD Player with a four CD changer. Plenty of room in the back if you have kids and a large boot for shopping and what not. Fancy a test drive?'

Here's a way that the salesman could have a lot more impact with his selling points. Consider how you would feel differently as the customer between the two approaches.

You're already on the test drive when the salesman begins:

Salesman: What sort of music do you tend to listen to when you're driving?

Customer: A mix of stuff really. I like Frank Sinatra and Elvis of course.

Salesman: Great, well this car has a CD player with a four-CD changer so you can leave your Elvis and Frank CD's in and flip between the two depending on what you fancy!

It's simple but effective. You probably just glanced over the fact that the car had a four-CD changer when you heard about it the first time because it wasn't applicable to you. Now it is applicable to the customer as an individual. Even the smaller selling points take on a whole new significance and can help you toward the sale. Already, the customer is imagining having their CDs on in the car as they drive along rather than the CD player being lost in a meaningless list of sales preamble.

Take a look at the differences between Unique Selling Points (USPs), features and benefits and then take some time to think about what you highlight about your company at the moment. Split the list into three for USPs, features and benefits and then try to add more now that you have this clear distinction. When you have your list clearly identified think of what questions you could ask your customer in order to get the selling points introduced that would make it applicable to them.

I'll talk more about meeting customer needs in the next section after clarifying the differences between, USPs, features and benefits.

11.1 USP's

A Unique Selling Point (USP) is something that your company offers, which <u>none</u> of your competitors do. It is something completely unique to your company that is of interest and benefit to the customer.

Sometimes the USP is the main reason the company was set up in the first place, i.e. the gap in the market or otherwise it is something that has been developed because it's a niche that you have found helps you win business. Either way – always highlight your USP's as the stand out features and benefits, ready to be put forward when the opportunity presents itself. Again, don't just go throwing your USP's away in the first sentence, they'll have less impact, though you should be looking for the right opportunity to get your major selling points in first, perhaps by asking fact-finding questions that guide the customer to talk about this area.

For instance, if your company had a unique medical procedure or pharmaceuticals that assisted arthritis you could ask, 'how do you currently treat arthritis?'. If you provided back-up storage for company's servers you could ask, 'how do you currently back up your data?' and 'how much does that cost?' before you present your innovative solution. Direct, fact-finding questions to get the customer talking about the specific area you wish to highlight. This way the solution becomes applicable to their situation.

It is true to say that a USP is only worthwhile if it does genuinely bring a unique *benefit* to your customer. 'A free sausage with every car bought' might well be unique but it probably won't sell many cars!

11.2 Features
These are the more standard selling points that you have to offer. Things that your competitors will also offer but benchmarks that you need to cover. 'Individually tailored quote', 'guaranteed next day delivery' etc. Not unique but definitely items that make you competitive and give good benefits to the customer. The example earlier of a '30 day money back guarantee' is most likely a feature as it may not

be something that a particular competitor does but others may well offer the same or very similar.

You can employ the same technique as above to get your features across, i.e. the appropriate question before any presentation. Bear in mind that you might not always get the answer that you are looking for! Features can also help alleviate any concerns your customer has or any basic questions they ask. E.g. answers to frequently asked questions are ready made features and benefits.

You should have a list of features as long as your arm ready for any objection you receive on the phone. If they have a concern or question, you have a remedy or answer to hand. Once again this is just good product knowledge being used to meet the customer's needs.

11.3 Benefits

A benefit is a by-product of a selling point or feature. E.g. Selling point – competitively priced; benefit – customer could save money. Selling point – largest range of products available; benefit – customer gets more choice and so on.

Take your list of USP's and features and identify the benefit to the customer. If you cannot think of a genuine benefit to the customer of a particular feature, then that particular feature probably isn't of any use to you, it if indeed should have been considered a feature at all.

In sales, it's often useful to lead with the benefit before the feature to arose the customer's interest. If you know that you can save the customer money you can highlight the benefit first, 'well if you're using Harry's Supplies at the moment you can most likely save a lot of money with us'. It's pretty obvious that they next question the customer will ask is for your prices. You can then get the specifics on what they buy and without too much pressure at all you've given them a direct quote! Being able to simply say, 'we can help you with that!' when someone presents an issue they're experiencing is tremendously effective. You can give them the benefit before the feature to further show that you are considering their perspective. It's the difference between the two sentences, 'you can save money with us' (customer's perspective) and 'we can save you money' (seller's perspective). Ideally you want to word the benefit that you are presenting to be from the customer's perspective.

Customer Focused Sales – checkpoint 3

Now we've considered all the aspects of our company's products and/or services we need to put them across to the client to match their situation. It is no use doing all this work in building an excellent rapport, listening with interest to what the customer has to say and then presenting the same solution or idea in the same way you do on every call. If you have got this far with a call you've really established the customer's interest in you and your company. Now the solution has to match. Let's look at how we meet the customer's needs that we've worked so hard to establish.

In the next chapter we're going to bring the call together by meeting the needs of the customer as presented in all the earlier chapters. Try to continue to think of the situation from the customer's point of view as we draw a line under our smiley car salesman example.

12.0 Meeting Customer's Needs

This is a good time to bring the theme together. We've now seen how to extract a lot of useful information from your customer and what we do with that information. The sales person who most effectively matches all their selling points to their customer's needs, will be the most effective sales person!

The whole point of all those questions and your list of USPs, features and benefits is to create a sales presentation to each customer that couldn't be better tailored in order to achieve a sale. This is the defining part of customer focused sales.

Let's go back to the car salesman. When we first saw this chap he had lots and lots to say about his 'car of the week' before learning a single thing about the customer. We gave him a nice open question to use to make the customer comfortable and to talk about their requirements and interests as much as possible. If the car salesman continued along the path described over the last few pages he would have learned more and more about the customer, able to ask fact-finding questions, 'what sort of journeys do you mainly use the car for?', 'what car's have you had previously that you liked?' (Just thought I'd throw a couple more examples in there!). With all this information the salesman would have been able to suggest the cars closest to the customer's requirements and within their budgets (meeting customer needs) and also been able to highlight further benefits to their situation. 'Your kids will really like this car too, it has lots of room in the back' can be said with much more confidence if the customer has said something like, 'I do the school run each day for my son and daughter'. This sentence is again from the customer's point of view, 'Your kids will really like this car too...' as opposed to, 'we find that this tends to be enough space for kids' or similar.

The more time you spend learning about your customer, the more features you would have matched to their situation and requirements. The more you manage to do this, the more likely you are to achieve a sale.

You should always be looking to ask yourself the following questions about your own approach: How would this approach work on me if I was the customer? Would I feel like I was being sold to or listened to?

And though we have now listened to our customer intently and tailored our services to match we have not quite got the deal sealed. You need to consider precisely what opportunities are in front of you and listen intently for any buying signals the customer may display before going in for the final task of getting the deal closed. Section C gives you lots of ideas for effective closers and you will see how these fit into your customer focused approached so that at no time during the call do we divert from this form of professional selling. First we'll have a look at what buying signals a customer might display and what opportunities we are likely to be presented with.

13.0 Buying signals

During the call you should be able to tell what level of interest the customer has in your services from their general demeanour – i.e. have they taken the time to speak to you etc. You can also look for key buying signals that indicate the likelihood of the sales call moving forward into something more significant. Here are a few key indicators that suggest the customer may have a requirement that you can meet and that they would be willing to do business with you.

1) They give you a lot of information about their current suppliers – someone who is trying to get you off the phone will simply say – 'we're covered for that thanks' or 'it's okay thanks, we use a local supplier'. Those who tell you who they use and about their orders or existing services are much more approachable for you to highlight your benefits and USPs to.

2) If the client is asking you questions about what you can do for them, they are obviously interested in at the very least comparing what you can offer with what they do in this particular area at the moment. This may be motivated by something simple such as saving money or by a particular area of concern that they have. This shouldn't be confused with a request for more general information, which could be being used just to end the conversation.

3) If the customer is asking about the credentials of your company they are likely to be interested in what you can do for them. A customer might want to know about the size of your company, how long you have been trading, your client history, your qualifications etc to ensure that you meet the standards they expect of their suppliers. If they are being dismissive they will not ask these questions but presume the negative, if they are asking you might feel temporarily under pressure but this is definitely a good thing. Imagine being on a date. You wouldn't ask about the other person's habits

and preferences if you thought that they were unattractive or dull would you?! If you found them attractive and pleasant on the service you would be keener to dig a little deeper and that is what's happening here.

4) Listen to the words that the customer is using. Utterances such as 'really?!' and 'that's interesting' may not sound quite the same as 'that sounds like exactly what I'm looking for – can I give you lots of money right now?!' but these sort of statements show that the customer is paying particular attention to what you're saying and that it is likely to fit into their situation. They are much stronger buying signals than simply 'yes' and 'okay' for instance.

5) A good level of rapport is a buying signal. We've talked about rapport and ultimately people buy from people. You are much more likely to sell to someone you get along well with. A good level of rapport allows you to be much more straight-forward about what you're looking to do because it won't just be construed as a sales pitch and therefore you are more likely to achieve your intended result. Remember that this level of rapport is built up, possibly over several conversations through discussing relevant things at length, the customer's requirements, displaying good product knowledge and talking about things affecting the sector at the moment etc. If a customer has indulged you for so long, they are likely to be keen to do business with you.

There are many more buying signals they we could go through but you will have a pretty good notion of when a call is going well and when it isn't so I'll leave the examples alone for the time being.

All the techniques discussed in this book so far help to get to this stage of the call where you will start to see the customer conveying buying signals. It's harder to come across buying signals that you haven't done a great amount of work to generate. All too often, from the people I have worked with, I hear people make a twenty second call after which they say, 'they weren't interested'. Of course they weren't interested! You only spoke to them for twenty seconds! It would take Jennifer Aniston to call me up and say, 'Hi, it's Jennifer Aniston. I'm free this evening if you're interested', for me to display buying signals after just twenty seconds! The aim of the call in the first twenty seconds is to make the call last a minute and when you've made it last a minute, to then make it last for five minutes and so on. You earn buying signals; they aren't just sat at the other end of the phone waiting for you to call! You should make every call with the knowledge that the person at the other end is not going to be interested in buying what you have unless you can sustain their interest over a period of time and use that time to understand as much about them as possible because then and only then can the customer's requirement be genuine.

The next step is to be clear about the opportunities that are in front of you. What does the customer want in the short term and long term? What are the specific additional benefits that they are after? Could they be a good point of repeat or referral business for you? How exactly are you going to win this business? We'll now look at the areas where you are likely to spot your best opportunities and then move on to the vital part of closing the deal!

14.0 Opportunity spotting

An owner of a shoe selling company took his two new sales people to the jungle for a training exercise. He sent each of them individually into the jungle to check for prospective shoe buyers. The first sales person walked into the jungle and came back many hours later. The boss asked what the prospects were like, 'terrible' said the first salesman, 'no-one in the jungle wears shoes'. The second salesman was sent into the jungle. He returned several hours later, 'How were the prospects?' asked the boss, 'excellent' replied the second sales person, 'no-one in the jungle wears shoes... yet!'.

The point of this little story is not that every sales person should be on a mission to change the requirements of their entire market or move into untouched markets etc. (I don't think jungle tribes people will have the adequate currency to complete the purchase of a nice pair of hush puppies). It's simply that what can seem like a barrier to one sales person, can be perceived as a potential opportunity to another. Throughout the call, particularly whilst your customer is talking you should be looking for areas to develop into opportunities and not looking for barriers or reasons to end the call. There will be both opportunities to highlight a USP, feature or benefit to the customer and opportunities for business beyond the obvious, initial purchase. In this section we will look at some examples of where you might find these.

14.1 Objections/concerns

As previously discussed, providing you have a good list of features and benefits, every 'objection' is an opportunity to present a positive selling point.

To handle an objection effectively – never say 'no' or 'but' to the objection. Replies such as 'I understand, that's important to a lot of our customers...', 'that's excellent and it's something we can help with...' and 'you're very right to be concerned about that and we have addressed these issues for our customers by...'. If you use language such as 'no' or 'but' you will begin to sound argumentative and it is not language that says *customer focused sales* to me. However, handled in the correct way objections can be opportunities to discuss the customer's concerns or areas of interest, which can steer the conversation towards what you can do for them.

Achieving a sale is never about winning a debate, it's about tuning in to your customer and getting what they want done for them. The customer is always right so when they have a concern it is for good reason. Of course you can hopefully dispel the concern and move them towards a purchase by endearing them towards your company. If you can solve issues they raise rather than dismiss or try to disprove them, you're onto a winner.

Objection handling is usually a much larger area of sales and telesales training. However, this needs to be specific to your company, i.e. what specific objections/concerns are you likely to come across and what is the best response to that. The basic formula is to present a feature or benefit and to keep the language positive, appreciating the customer's position. Patiently handling an objection, which has a positive outcome, is a fantastic rapport builder.

14.2 Competitors

Never be put off by a customer mentioning a competitor. I've seen telesales staff hear the mention of a competitor, 'we use XYZ recruitment ', and reply, 'erm, okay, thanks for your time anyway'. In most instances the customer will already use someone to provide the same, or at least very similar services, to what you offer. Your task is to see how you can contribute additional benefits to the products or services that they already use.

It is advisable to take a good look at your competitors and understand your position in the marketplace. The more you know about the companies whom you are up against, the stronger a pitch you can make to a potential customer.

There are two types of competitor you need to be aware of:

14.2.1 Direct competition.

These are competitors who sell what you sell to who you sell it i.e. they do what you do. Coca-cola is in direct competition with Pepsi in the same way that two financial recruitment agencies in Manchester are in direct competition. These will be the companies that your potential customers mention most regularly when you are speaking to them about your specific products and services, who they already use and/ or who they are considering using next.

14.2.2   Indirect competition

These are companies who can provide an alternative solution to your target market. i.e. same target audience, different angle. In this instance Coca-cola would consider Evian water and Lucozade (GlaxoSmithKlein) competition. Rather than convincing people to choose your cola instead of a rival's cola, you are trying to convince them to drink cola over water or something else.

14.2.3   Competitor SWOT analysis

A great exercise to find out more about your competitors is to look them up online and do a SWOT (strengths, weaknesses, opportunities, threats) analysis from what they advertise about themselves.

i.e. What do they do well?

What do they offer that you don't?

What don't they offer that you do?

Where are they based?

What accreditations do they have and how does that compare to yours?

What are their prices like compared to yours?

Do they have a prestigious client base?

How long have they been trading?

Example:

Strengths	Weaknesses
• Long trading history • Some major clients • Good accreditations • National coverage	• Fairly expensive • Only operate in certain sectors • Narrow range of services
Opportunities	Threats
• Highlight pricing as major advantage – customer can save money • Target less competitive sectors to win higher proportion of business • Offer full range of services to be more comprehensive and competitive	• Trading history may make going for larger contracts more difficult • Need to expand on current accreditations • Difficult to compete for non-local custom

This is a generic example just to illustrate the layout and the purpose. A competitor's strengths are a threat to you winning business from them and their weaknesses are potential opportunities for you to highlight and exploit. You simply need to concentrate on your strengths and opportunities and do not dwell on your weaknesses or threats. SWOT tables are usually drawn in this way. You might wish to swap the opportunities box with the threats box so that the bottom two boxes lie directly beneath the corresponding top box.

Even if you only do this with your main competitors whose name's you regularly hear from your customers you can have ideas ready to mention as in the earlier examples. The main reason for repeating the point here is to emphasise that hearing a competitor's name is a genuine opportunity and something you can easily be prepared for. When someone makes a sales call and hears a competitor's name, it is very easy to see that as a barrier. In the short term it possibly is but it certainly isn't in the long term. Have you ever changed your mobile phone, Internet, gas and/or electricity provider etc because of poor service or due to a change in circumstances? I'm sure you have. Being with British Gas doesn't stop Scottish Power sending you information about their services does it? And if one could save you money or you get poor service from your current supplier you would likely change, would you not?

Don't be put off by your competitors - they are there for the taking. Do you think your competitors would try and take over contracts you have? I'm sure they would. So long as you don't resort to aggressive tactics and remain customer focused in your approach, there is a lot of business to be won off the back of finding out who the customer currently uses and of course highlighting the advantages of using your company. Basically, when the customer mentions a competitor you have learned a bit more about them, which should help and not hinder.

14.3 Long term opportunities

You should always have both your short and long term goals in mind. Short term opportunities are those which will help you make a sale today. Long term opportunities are those which lie beyond the initial sale. Some sales people fall down by concentrating on one or the other.

Short term focused only - If you only concentrate on getting short term business, i.e. a sale there and then and then move onto the next customer whether the last one bought or not you are certainly not making the most of the potential that every client has. Over time each customer could do more for your business than the next few hundred cold calls that you make.

Long term focused only - Some sales people unwittingly use their long term focus as an excuse for not closing the business in the short term, operating a consistent cycle of 'calling back in three months' or similar. If you only concentrate on the long term it can cause huge cash-flow problems for your business. You wouldn't wait until next quarter for your wages would you? Though the focus of this book is on the customer, ultimately what we're trying to do is be profitable for the business owner, so we should spare them at least a small amount of sympathy!!

The best balance you can achieve is to be determined to get the short term sale, i.e. turn the customer into a client, even if that initial sale isn't the biggest sale you will ever achieve with that client. Converting a potential customer from being a 'prospect' to become a paying 'client' is the biggest hurdle you have in sales. This is where the 'pipeline' group of customers is crucial is storing all those customers who you will concentrate on converting into 'clients' in the short term. We are going to look at closing techniques shortly. The long term opportunities can be focused on once they become 'clients'.

Long term opportunities include:

Repeat business – where the client comes back to purchase again in the future.

Increased business – where the client's orders grow over time to become larger and/or more regular.

Referral business – where the client recommends you to other people who could benefit from your services.

Leverage business – where you use your client's name to leverage more business in that particular sector. (For instance, if you were trying to sell GPS services to logistics companies, getting the first logistics company on board would be hugely beneficial for you long term as you could mention the name(s) of the company(s) you were providing these services to and this would increase the confidence in your services if a name known in that sector was using you). The question here then is, is the customer going to be good for name dropping or for proving the concept?

Keeping these long term goals in mind can help you keep strong motivation to get that first initial sale and not let a potential gold-mine pass you by.

14.4 Referrals

Referral business is the most effective way to grow your client base. I'll say that again. Referral business is the most effective way to grow your client base. After all, why would you want to spend all your time selling if other people are doing it for you? If your job is full time sales, having people who refer strong prospects into you is like having more time on the phone that you otherwise just wouldn't have.

If you come highly recommended from either someone who already uses you or from a source you have within an advice network, the leads you receive are very warm unlike the cold leads we were calling at the start of this book. They are warm because they have some kind of requirement you could possibly meet and you have come via a network and not called out of the blue so they will be more willing to listen to and trust you. That recommendation is worth its weight in gold in terms of how you prove your worth. If you have to convince a customer that you are what you say you are, you are going to have a much harder time than you would if an existing customer or other referee has done it for you.

This is why, when you go to the gym, near enough every month they will have 'bring a friend for free' day or when you join a membership website there is always a 'recommend a friend' button.

Look at the following two sentences and ask yourself what are the different effects that you feel and therefore what effect would this have on a potential customer?

- Bill's Restaurant - We have great food and great service and are the best restaurant in town!

How does that sound? What does it make you think/feel?

- I went to Bill's Restaurant the other day. Both the food and service was fantastic, it's easily the best restaurant in town!

How about this one? Obviously, we have to talk our businesses up and install some enthusiasm and belief in our customers but sometimes that sales pitch or recommendation coming from a third party who have experienced it for themselves just cannot be beaten. The more of these referees you have in place the better. The more existing customers who sing your praises, the more new customers you are likely to acquire. This is why lots of companies have customer testimonials on their website. They are not showing off but advertising their business in the third person and basically saying, don't just take our word for it!

So, how can you use this in your telesales? Each time you complete a transaction for a customer ask them, 'do you know of anyone else who may benefit from our services?'. Ask every time because even a happy client isn't that likely to go out of their way to get other people to use you. Some companies offer referral commissions to encourage their clients to refer people on a regular basis. Your company might not do this but this is not the critical part. Pro-actively asking your customers for referrals is the critical part because if every customer gave you the number of someone else who bought you might never need to make a cold-call again! Okay, the likelihood of that is a slight exaggeration but it certainly increases the number of warm leads you have to call (or get called by) each day.

14.4.1 Calling a Referred Lead

Here's an example of how to emphasise the referral for maximum effectiveness on a call whilst remaining a customer focused sales person:

You recently designed Bob's website. Bob is an ice cream wholesaler and recommends Joe who runs the logistics company that delivers for Bob. Bob gives you Joe's number so you call Joe and can form your introduction around that. Remember that the aim of your introduction is still to sound interesting and professional so you might introduce yourself to Joe along these lines:

'Good afternoon Joe. This is John Smith calling from Smith Designs. Bob Jones asked me to give you a call as we recently designed his website and he mentioned that you were also looking at getting a website done for yourself. Is now a good time to talk about what you're looking for?... That's great, well, tell me more about your business and the website you're thinking of...' Of course you can feel free to include the usual 'how are you?' and so on.

Note how we've been able to get the customer to feel trusted in us because of why we've phoned and have still gone for a nice open question, 'tell me more about your business and the website you're thinking of...', how long could Joe potentially talk for based on this opening question and how much information might you gather from that? We do this regardless of the information Bob provided us with as you need to hear all about the business and what they're looking for directly from the customer in order to meet his requirements specifically as well as highlight your USP's features and benefits as to make them appropriate to the customer. Bob's referral also gives you leverage. 'Bob was very pleased with the customer enquiry form we added to his website', 'we did Bob a great price on his website so I'm sure we'll be able to give you a great deal too' etc.

A great project to undertake to add a boost to your current sales is to go back through your client base and try and generate some referral business. With your boss' permission, phone every single client you have simply as a courtesy. If they haven't bought from you in a while find out when they are likely to place their next order (repeat business) or if they have any issues that need sorting and once you have addressed everything from their point of view ask if they know of anyone who could benefit from your services (referral business). Free sales and recommendations – it's a no-brainer as they say.

Section C
<u>Getting Down To Business</u>

Section C – Getting Down to Business

Nice marketing and chatting to customers is all well and good but unless you close the deal you've still not achieved anything. It's a bit like a Venus Fly Trap with Lock-jaw!

In this section we are going to look at how to call a customer to action and actually produce the result that we set out to achieve. Whether you are looking to book a sales appointment or closing the deal over the phone you need to be ready to get your customer across the crucial line to become a client. This will hopefully be a continuation of your 'follow up' call. Though this is a separate section, I'm not suggesting you make a new call when you've just done so much to build the customer's interest.

15.0 The Sales Presentation

This book can be read by and helpful to people selling any product or service and by this stage of the call conversations can take so many tangents that it would be either impossible or wrong for me to give you the 'right' way or even a good way to present your business. It depends what you are selling and who you are selling it to.

Here I will give you one key phrase that will help you when you come to convince the customer that now is the time to act and to buy what you are selling, be that a further sales meeting or making the purchase there are then and in the next two chapters I will provide further tips for getting them to say 'yes' when you begin to ask your closing questions.

When you are ready to call your customer to action, i.e. when you have asked all the questions you possibly could have, fully understood the customer's requirements, built a good level of rapport, handled objections professional and positively and you are certain you have a solution that is suitable (or hopefully ideal) for the customer, use the techniques below but lead them into this with the phrase:

'What I can do for you is....'.

You are not telling the customer what your company does, you are not telling the customer what they should do, you are not even telling the customer that you are going to do something that you don't yet have their permission for. You are personalising the whole situation that you have been building on for the last however many calls and minutes. Use the sentence, 'what I can do for you is...' followed by the solution you are thinking of and possibly linked with some of the closing techniques coming up. It is the perfect customer focused sales sentence. You are personally taking ownership of all your customer's requirements. They are now personally in your hands and you are helping them get what they want and improve their situation.

Customer Focused Sales checkpoint 4

I can't stress enough how important it is not to let this method of selling slip at any time.

If you were the customer and had had someone take so much time to learn all about your situation, you'd got along well with them and you were interested in buying, how disappointed would you be with the sales person if they used a phrase such as:

'what you should probably do is...' or;

'what we usually do is...'

When you are speaking to someone regarding a problem be it your bank, doctor, boss or other and you require a bit of help, how much do you crave to hear the words, 'what I can do for you is...'?

This is very powerful in getting your customer to make that commitment because they are then doing it for them and not for you or anyone else. You are just there to help. When you call one of your own existing providers with a customer service enquiry you really appreciate it when someone takes ownership of the situation and works hard to help you. You can easily apply this to your sales and it is very effective.

16.0 Appointment Setting

Those of you who operate in a business to business market in particular will know that very little gets bought directly over the phone (definitely not new services, that's for sure). All this work and your short-term goal is just an appointment! However, don't be deterred! I'm sure that you are targeted on the number of appointments you generate and on the business gained from those appointments and all these techniques will of course just mean that you book more and more, good quality appointments so that whether it's you or one of your field sales personnel that attends the appointment, you can go well prepared to provide that customer with exactly what they are looking for.

If you are targeted to generate sales appointments then here's a great closer that shows flexibility and professionalism whilst being effective and so will help you achieve that short term aim.

16.1 Get it 'pencilled' in

This is a nice phrase to use when looking to book an initial appointment. 'Can we get something pencilled in for next week?'. Using a closing question to get the customer to make a commitment to have an appointment but in quite a relaxed manner. This is particularly useful when people are avoiding an appointment because of their busy schedule. If you say 'call me back when you are free for an appointment', you might well be waiting quite some time for that call. If you know that there is a need there that you can meet, it pays to be proactive before that need is met by someone else!

Example: 'Can we get something pencilled in for next week?... Whenever you have a gap in your diary at the moment... I will give you a call the day before just to check that nothing has come up and that you will still be available... we look forward to seeing you next Tuesday.'

You have demonstrated that you do not wish to be a burden on your customer's time and that you respect that their day job comes before meeting you in order to discuss buying something that might not be time urgent. This is a very professional approach that allows you to get a commitment from the customer because you are offering flexibility. The key is to get them to make a note in their diary. If you call back the day before and they have too much on you can put the meeting back in the diary by a few days. You still have the commitment, you're already meeting a need on behalf of the customer and you maintain patience and professionalism that will ultimately help you close the deal. A moved appointment is much better than no appointment or the 'promise' of one in the future.

16.2 Meeting brief

When you have booked an appointment ensure that you pass all the information you have gathered onto your field sales person. If you are attending the sales meeting yourself, this is a lot easier because it was you who had all the previous conversations and so knows the customer's situation pretty well. If it isn't you, then you need to fill the field sales person in on everything you know about that customer, as if he or she had made all the calls.

Some field sales people can have a bit of a one-track mind and use a particular approach in every sales meeting but the information you have gathered on the phone is vital to that meeting so don't let the appointment be attended without all the information you have being known. Quite often the customer will only agree to a sales meeting because they have a high level of interest based on something you've discussed on the phone so you've basically made the sale and the field sales person is there to put a face to the company and dot the 'i's and cross the 't's as they say.

Your database or CRM may be able to produce template documents for each time you book an appointment. It will generate a sheet with all the address and contact details on for the customer and you can then paste all your notes onto this and pass it along to the field sales person. You then have a documented copy of each appointment made, rather than just a diary note so you can keep track of all the feedback from those meetings much easier.

Here's an example, similar to what I have used in the past for clients in the logistics sector:

Appointment Date	Monday 3rd November
Appointment Time	14:00pm
Name	Percy Winton
Position	Warehouse Manager
Company	ABC Manufacturing
Sector	Toys & Games
Address	Unit 7, Langthwaite Industrial Estate, London, NW19 1TP
Contact number	0208 769 4355
Email	percy.winton@abc-manufacturing.com
Number of Pallets moved per week	20-25
Current suppliers	XYZ Logistics
Received intro literature	Yes, company brochure & weblink, via email
Notes	Mainly boxed board games taken on wrapped pallets. 20-25 per week on average though very busy at the minute in run up to Christmas. John is a QPR fan and recently came back from a holiday in Spain.

How well prepared would the sales person be if they were to walk into a meeting armed with all this knowledge? They can have an excellent idea about pricing before they go in because the know about the number of pallets usually moved, the can instantly start to build rapport by talking about football or asking about the holiday that the customer recently went on. He could even have a prepared strategy to offer to help with the extra pallets up to Christmas in order to get the initial sales done and prove their worth as a logistics company by offering a short term contract in the first instance (more on the closing techniques in the next chapter).

If you were going to a sales appointment, how much do you think a brief like this would help you prepare for that meeting and be confident of winning the business versus just having a name and time to visit with very little other information?

You can easily create a template like this for your business, one that will massively help the field sales person close more business and possibly earn you more commission! You need to include all contact details you have for that person, details of what they have received from you, vital consumer information (what size of their orders are likely to be), competitor details, your field sales person is likely to be aware of the strengths and weaknesses of their competitors and anything that will help you field sales person build extra rapport with the customer, interests, holidays, details about their current situation. Your company will stand out from the crowd of people quoting for that business based on the relationship between your sales person and the decision maker above most other aspects. Don't allow all the good rapport you've developed during your sales calls to be extinguished because someone else is now taking over the relationship, allow them to pick up where you left off as this will ultimately help your customer (they don't have to go over things twice) and your company (more sales!).

Customer Focused Sales – checkpoint 5

Take a moment to imagine being the person who the appointment has been booked with. You spent a fair bit of time on the phone and agreed to have somebody visit your workplace, so several things can be safely assumed here.

- You have a requirement for the products or services being discussed

- You got along well with the person on the phone

- You gave the person on the phone an indication about your company's requirements and your own preferences

- You have already asked specific questions and discussed possible objections

Now if the person you were speaking to on the phone was called Betty and the sales person attending the appointment is called Norman, what are you expecting of Norman?

You would have expected him to have been briefed on what has already been discuss and done an amount of research on your company and have some information and example quotes prepared. This is why it is vitally important to have a good communication with your field sales staff, because all your hard work in information gathering and rapport building can be rapidly undone by a sales person who ignores all that work and makes the customer start from scratch again.

You would be expected to be treated as an individual. This is a customer who you have worked to develop a good relationship with. Hammer home the point that this is not to be wasted!

16.3 Inbound lead generation

Quite often, with the inbound sales people I have worked with, it is their job to secure providing the customer with a quote for another service with you, whether you provide the quote or pass the call to a colleague to arrange it. This usually starts after you've dealt with the customer's initial enquiry and you try and then direct the call toward a sale before the customer ends the call. For instance you might say, 'whilst you're on the line...' and ask them about their current gas supplier or Internet provider or whatever you sell. A couple of useful tips: One, avoid the closed question to steer the conversation. 'Whilst I have you on the phone, do you have a minute to talk about your Internet service?' The answer to this, more often than not will be, 'No, sorry I'm very busy', mainly because they want to avoid being sold to. So, we need to help the customer choose to buy (or receive the quotation at the very least). 'Whilst I've got you on the phone, if you have a brief moment I can see if we can save you some money on your Internet service.' If the customer is really busy, they can still disengage from the conversation but you are not encouraging this by asking an unnecessary closed question.

Tip two, is to emphasise the fact that this is a free quote with no obligation to buy and therefore the customer can only save money. It's okay to be slightly less formal here and appeal to the customer's ability to think logically. If it's only going to take a moment and the worst case scenario is that it isn't cheaper or better in any way then he/she doesn't change. Straight forward enough. Also see chapter 16.2 on presumptive closing to further support this.

17.0 Closing techniques

It is at this stage that we start to employ 'closing questions'. We are looking for the customer to make some sort of commitment. You have taken a lot of time to consider the individual customer, presented your company as tailored to them and addressed any concerns or objections and they have shown some buying signals. We now need to secure the result as intended from the very beginning. It is no good being a customer focused sales person if you are not effective at closing deals, otherwise you're just customer services!

Throughout this book we've heard the customer say very little. This is due to the fact that were you to attempt to predict what the customer might say you would either be preparing for something that was unlikely to happen or this book would rival War and Peace in its substance. The entire book however is geared to getting the customer to say one word.... 'yes'!

Even if your close is to secure a further sales appointment for a colleague, you still need to use closing techniques to get them over the line. The techniques in chapter 15 are specific to appointment setting but the techniques in this chapter can be used to close the deal, whether that's a sale or an appointment. You can use a combination of these techniques to help you close a deal.

See if you can identify techniques you already use, whether you do it deliberately or not.

17.1 Multiple Choice closing

This is where you come to get your client to make a decision and rather than presenting them with a 'yes/no' option, you present them with an 'A or B (and also perhaps C)' option. For instance, rather than asking, 'would you like to buy the car today?', which is a 'yes/no' option, you present the client with two options and ask, 'would you prefer the Vauxhall Corsa or Ford Focus?'. You might well know which car is more suitable to the customer and which car they are 99% certain to choose but this is still a great way of presenting the customer with choice so that they feel like they are buying and not being sold to, as well as significantly reducing your chances of a 'no'.

I have found that customers, quite rightly, always like to have their say. If their moment of input is to make a yes/no decision, 'yes' or 'no' they shall choose. If they have an 'A' or 'B', they are more likely to weigh up the pros and cons of the two options and therefore much less likely to opt for 'no'.

If you are appointment setting and you feel that you are on the brink of booking an appointment you can present multiple options to your customer again, rather than give them chance to make an excuse. 'Is this week or next week better for a meeting?' is far more likely to get a meeting booked into the diary than, 'would you like an appointment then?' This brings us nicely to our next closing technique, *presumptive closing.*

17.2 Presumptive closing

If you've had an excellent chat with the customer, they have displayed buying signals and you've found an excellent solution for them, it is beneficial to maintain an air of confidence through which you proceed to move things forward until the customer says differently. If the customer says something along the lines of, 'yes, I'd be interested in learning more about what you do?', proceed to booking an appointment, i.e. confirming dates etc because if you keep double checking that the customer would like an appointment you can seem less professional and give them plenty of chance to say 'no'.

There is a joke about Jehovah's Witnesses not knowing what to do when someone actually invites them into their home for a chat! This is because they are so used to people saying 'no', they adopt a presumption that even someone who has expressed some interest will still ultimately turn them away (or so the joke suggests!).

If you walk up to the counter in McDonalds, they ask, 'can I take your order please?'. You've walked up to the counter of an eatery so they presume you are going to order something. How much business do you think McDonalds would lose if their counter staff started asking, 'are you sure you want to order some food?!' several times. There's no reason to keep giving people chance to change their mind to your disadvantage, also being a customer focused sales person would dictate that you honour your customer's wishes and carry on. Questioning their decision or putting doubts in their mind is not only counter-productive but also a cause for concern to the customer. Therefore, maintain a confident air at all times to help get the deal completed.

Throughout the sales process it is important not to make any assumptions about your customer, each is unique of course, however carrying the confidence of someone who regularly sells is far more beneficial than repeatedly re-affirming the customer's interest.

The psychology here is that if you act like someone who is not 100% confident about what you are selling the customer will assume that there is something to be concerned about and begin to have second thoughts. If you walk them through the sales process with no hesitation, they will have more confidence in what you are providing and in you as a sales person. So, instead of 'would you be interested in having a meeting?' after a long and positive discussion the phrase, 'I'm free next Wednesday, is that a good day for you?' is far more effective. You could even use a fact-finding question as part of your closing for this technique and ask, 'when would be a good time to get together to look at some pricing for you?'. This works providing it isn't a rushed statement after a few minutes of speaking on the phone and if instead it is a statement said in a friendly way to a person that you have developed a good level of rapport with. It is a technique, which can back-fire to make you sound arrogant and presumptuous if used too early.

The next few closing techniques are all different areas of your USP's, features and benefits that you can emphasise in order to get a 'yes'.

17.3 Customer agreement

A very useful clinching closing question to use is, rather than saying, 'would you like to buy today?', to go for a closing question that gets the customer to agree with you rather than feel as if they are being sold to. Examples of this are:

'Does that sound like a good idea?'

'Do you think that that could be of benefit to you?'

Or even the more open:

'How does that sound?'

I would recommend using the closing questions as being the most effective to call your customer to action, though I always like to suggest flexibility and natural speech in your approach and therefore something along the lines of, 'how does that sound?' can still be very effective. This type of questioning partners particularly well with the earlier mentioned key sentence, 'what I can do for you is...'. Listen to this through, 'what I can do for you is.... does that sound like a good idea?'. How effective do you think that could be? How easy does that sound to say 'yes' to?

17.4 Fear of loss

This is particularly useful if your sales pitch revolved around any of the following:

- Special offer for a limited time only

- Limited amount of stock/low availability

- Something their competitors are taking advantage of

    or can give them a competitive edge

- One-off item that is only being offered to several people.

People often buy on impulse, even if they later justify this emotion with the logic of the benefit(s) that they have received. If people are instilled with a 'fear of loss' they will react quicker. Emphasising the possible loss of benefits to the customer without them acting quickly, increases your chances of a 'yes'. The focus of the 'fear of loss' technique is very much short-term so do bear this in mind if you are speaking to a client who has excellent long-term possibilities. In which case this might not be the best technique to concentrate on.

This is the sort of technique used by furniture shops when they have their 'Big Sale Weekends' to make you think that you'll never see that price again. Usually the offers are back on a week later so please note, I do only encourage this where the offer is genuinely limited stock or for a limited period.

17.5 Return on Investment

Depending on what you are selling you may be able to present a good return on investment for your client. This is possible if you sell any amount of advertising, marketing, web-design, recruitment and so on. If the client is likely to gain a good return by using you emphasis the expected figures and providing these are based on real examples and accurately calculated predictive the client will again be instilled with a 'fear of loss' emotion.

For instance, if you offer a money saving solution for your customer, emphasise the return. Imagine that you are suggesting a new phone system to a company with quite a few employees. 'A thousand pound spend should save you approximately five thousand over the next twelve months...' Real life case studies are much more important than theory here. The customer will want to know that what you're saying is proven and not just speculation, otherwise it is simply a risk and a gamble to them. Being able to say, 'we saved Jim's Pet Store over two thousand pounds last year and he runs a similar size business to yours' has the effect you're looking for rather than the inclusion of 'hopefully', 'should', 'approximately' or even worse, 'in theory'!

17.6 Two-way Street

Could your company use your client's services at any time in the future or are you in a network that could benefit the customer? In business-to-business sectors companies often supply to one another as a matter of loyalty, having a good business relationship and to help themselves gain that contract in the first place.

Are there any opportunities that you can think of? The customer is then more likely to initiate the business relationship as they will be more eager to build the long term relationship. Much like the return on investment, the blow of paying out money is softened by the long term potential of the transaction.

Again, this is something to emphasise only if the opportunities are genuine and this is not a regular option. You cannot become a client of every one of your clients nor can you spend your time promoting them all. Look to your current suppliers for these opportunities so that you are then looking to sell rather than buy.

17.7 Easy-in Easy-out

Trial periods, short term contracts, money back guarantee, flexible options. All these things are devices companies put in place to ease customers into the deal. No-one likes to make a long term commitment to a company that they haven't tried out and so these things are very beneficial for helping close a deal. If your company then delivers all that you were suggesting you would be able to deliver you keep that client long term.

The easy-in/easy-out system gets them over that vital first hurdle. If your company offers anything like this, emphasise it at the point of sale. 'Don't just take my word for it, let's get you signed up for one month and you can see for yourself. If you don't feel like you've had the sort of service you were expecting you can simply end the contract after thirty days at no additional cost. However, the vast majority of people stay with us far beyond their trial period, I can assure you!'. This sort of language, levitates the pressure of the decision at the critical point, you can also see how this language is presumptive and confident. If you are confident that you have provided your customer with a great deal to suit them this confidence will rub off on the customer and they will have a lot more confidence in using you.

This is essentially the opposite of the return on investment. Rather than emphasising what a customer could possibly gain, you are emphasising what they don't stand to lose. The example above regarding the telephone system could be emphasised as, 'why not trial the system free for one month? If we can't prove that there will be long term savings we will remove the system and you would have spent nothing.' This may not be a viable for a company to actually provide but if the system does work it's a great tactic as most customers will keep the system to make the savings. From the customer's point of view, it's also very difficult to say 'no' to because there's practically nothing to lose.

Once again, these are ideas that you can use to help you complete that call and seal the deal. Do take these ideas and develop them to suit you, they are not set in stone. They need to work both for your company and what it provides as well as you as an individual. Good luck!

Section D
<u>You The Sales Person</u>

Section D – You the salesperson

In this final section we will take some time to look at the auxiliary functions of being a sales person. i.e. those things which you need to consider which are not you speaking to a customer.

Telesales can be a difficult job both technically and at times emotionally, when things aren't going your way. I really enjoy telesales and have had much success on many projects, though I don't consider myself immune to such things. Hopefully all the techniques in the previous three sections have given you lots of ideas to take forward and helped boost your confidence that you are capable of improving your results on the phone. If I ended the book here I would be doing all telesales people a disservice because as I've mentioned previously, there is no magic trick or simple solution to making telesales work but you can be great at it and thoroughly enjoy it with the right approach, lots of hard work and a dedication to professionalism.

I hope this final chapter ties things together for you and answers a few questions you may have been thinking whilst reading this book.

18.0 Keeping a customer on the phone

At this juncture, I'd just like to take a moment to touch on something that quite a few people I train get hung up on (no pun intended). As mentioned earlier in the book, there is nothing to stop people being short with or rude to you if they feel that way inclined. However, the techniques presented in this book are designed to keep the customer talking, to pay attention to them and to build and build on the business relationship from day one.

You will find that people are a lot more ready and willing to discuss things with you over the phone when presented with this sort of professional approach. Having said this, this does not change the reality of people not being available when you call, people being sceptical about your claims or people generally being busy and not having all the time in the world to chat. This 'follow up call' may well be three or four calls spread out over three or four weeks, such is business. Don't let this get you down! You now clearly have a goal and tactics in mind. Stick with them and they will pay dividends. Do not be too downhearted if you fail to keep a customer on the phone for ten minutes with each call, it can't be done every time.

19.0 Motivation

Okay, now you know loads and loads of things that can be used throughout your call to help you help the customer and bring more business into your company. All well and good, however, we still know that telesales can be a cruel game and that rude people and weeks that bring poor results can massively affect your motivation and confidence so this needs addressing for everyone who gets involved with sales. I've done lots of telesales and more often than not have achieved excellent results but that does not mean that I haven't had moments where I wanted to swear at people at the other end of the phone, throw the phone out of the window or spend half an hour surfing the Internet to give me a break from making calls. Here are some tips to maintain your motivation to keep picking the phone up with a cheery smile.

1) First and foremost – ask yourself this small series of questions:

    Do you believe in what you are selling?

    Do you feel that you can sincerely help the customer?

    What is your company's mission statement?

    What does the company want to do to help your clients?

    Do you believe in the company's vision?

In life you are motivated by your beliefs and values. E.g. You are motivated to be kind to people because you believe that it is the right thing to do, even on days where you might not feel at your most polite and friendliest. You need to weave the company's dream into your own belief system by fully understanding the goals of the company. Those who do, love to sell their products and services and those who don't feel like they have to lie through gritted teeth during their sales calls. It is about believing that every time you speak to someone about your company you are genuinely looking help them in some way. Being a customer focused sales person will mean that those who are rude to you have made a mistake in thinking that you were another hard-nosed sales person. Those who then choose to ignore you have missed out and you can move on to the next call with the same belief still intact.

2)   Decide on some goals both long and short term:

For instance – short term – 'get 3 deals every week' and long term – 'to become the top sales person in the company'. Write these goals down. It might sound simple but writing goals down makes you more committed to them and each time you see them they will boost your motivation. There is an article from my website in the appendix of this book, which expands on the idea of goal setting and its benefits.

3)   Use your database to your advantage:

Earlier we talked about how to organise your data into groups on your database (if you didn't do something similar to this already) but you can also use this to divide up your day in order to keep you motivated. For example, each day you will have important follow up calls to make. These will most likely be to people who are categorised as 'prospects' and 'pipeline'. Prioritise these and the times of day you feel that you are most likely to get hold of them or they have asked you to call back. Then decide how many 'suspects' you are going to call between these times. By breaking down these introductory calls into maybe groups of five or ten, it feels more organised than just starting ringing through a list that you are going to be ringing through all day. Monotony diffuses motivation so break your day into segments to help keep your focus.

4)   Self-train:

If you work in a team of sales people ask someone to listen to your calls. You might have a sales manager that does this already but if you don't it is beneficial to exchange this exercise with a colleague. Listen to one another's calls and make suggestions to one another about what else could have been said/asked to help the call along. Helping other people with their calls helps you with your own and you can always be looking to make improvements to find what works for you.

5)   Remind yourself of the good times:

One thing that tends to liquidate motivation is the repeat 'no's that you get over the phone. People who do not want to buy from you for one reason or another. Remind yourself of the success you have had by placing your best results above your desk. Your biggest client, most deals done in a month, most money banked in a quarter or your equivalent. This not only gives you something to aim for but also reminds you that you are good at your job and of what you can achieve. You are focusing on the positive and not the negative, which may have just occurred on the phone. I simply keep my client's cards posted above my desk to remind me of the good work I do and have done for them, then if I'm looking for new work I have that inspiration to draw on.

6)   If you don't shoot you won't score!

I do enjoy my football analogies so please humour me if you're not a football fan! If you're not on the phone you won't sell. Motivation enough in itself perhaps? As a telesales person, not being on the phone talking to potential and existing customers is a drain on your company's finances and the one thing that will definitely lead to poor results, which takes us on quite nicely to our next topic.

20.0   Quality versus Quantity

I've worked in sales offices where managers constantly scream, 'make more calls, make more calls!'. To achieve the very best results possible what they should be shouting is, 'be on the phone more, be on the phone more!'.

Most people will tell you that sales is a numbers game and to an extent it is. What some people don't realise is that just focusing on quantity, i.e. as many calls in a day as possible, isn't necessarily going to achieve the best results.

Being on the phone is much better than not being on the phone, that is for certain, however, I always tell my staff, 'if you're going to be on the phone for ten minutes, I'd rather that it was one ten minute call than five calls under two minutes'. That's because if call one has lasted ten minutes you're getting a lot closer to achieving a sale and building a relationship with that customer than you possibly could on a two minute call. The second, third, fourth calls will all be there when you're done with call one so don't rush a potential customer off the phone in order to make more calls!

There is a positive correlation between the number of calls a sales person makes and the number of sales they get. There is a much more positive correlation between the amount of *time* someone spends on the phone and the sales they achieve. If Geoff makes 100 calls and is on the phone for a total of 500 minutes and Steve makes 150 calls and is on the phone for a total of 300 minutes, who is more likely to have made the most sales?

All the techniques in this book will make your calls last longer, give you the ability to learn much more about your customer and achieve much better long and short term results.

When you're not on the phone – make another call. When you're on the phone, make the call count!

21.0 Scripting

This section could possible have come earlier in the book and probably would have if I was of the nature to believe that a strict script is the way to go. The worst telesales people of all are those who just sound scripted. I even prefer it when I get and automated message of some kind because at least they've cut out the middle man and just employed a robot, rather than employ a human to act like one. Having said this, the majority of people who work in telesales do prefer to have prompts around to help ensure that they don't miss any vital information, if they do get stuck on what to say they have a reminder to hand and saying certain things in the same way may well build your confidence and reduce the risk of sounding unsure on the phone.

Think again of the Chief Executive of a bank making a call. We looked at an introduction he might make. He sounded very professional but not at all scripted. If you are a true professional you should know your products and/or services well enough not to need to read a script over the phone. You should be confident enough in your own ability to discuss what you are selling even if you keep just a few pointers to hand.

For each project I've worked on and all those people who I've set working on different projects, I've always done a basic 'script' for, just to provide a template and guide to the call but for Pete's sake, please do not just read a script verbatim!

Here's what I usually put in a 'script':

- Introduction and good opening question
- List of open and fact-finding questions, which link to the vital data capture
- List of USPs, features & benefits
- Example call to action (preferred closing question)

Here's an example for the auto-parts company we were using earlier:

Intro:

Good Morning, my name is John Smith calling from Jolly Rogers Auto-parts. We supply quality spares to automotive retailers. I am looking to find out more about the products you sell and possibly provide someone with one of our brochures today. Who would be best to speak to?

Questions:

Tell me about your current stock?

Which suppliers do you use currently?

What is your current turnover on this type of product?

When are you next due to review your product range?

How regularly do you order new stock?

USPs, Features & Benefits

Competitively priced

30 day money back guarantee

Wide range of products

Nationwide next day delivery

Phone and internet orders

New catalogue every six months

No minimum order unlike a lot of competitors

Call to Action

Would you like to place an order?

Do also feel free to include key phrases such as, 'what I can do for you is...' but nothing too extensive. Even having the introduction written down will become redundant once you are used to the new format.

There is nothing here to make you sound robotic or rigid, they're just pointers. Very useful if you get stuck or can't remember what you were going to ask because you've been distracted by the conversation you were having. There's not a lot that's more annoying than having a really good conversation with a potential customer and coming off the phone and suddenly realising you've missed a vital question that they would have been happy to answer and would have helped you with the sale and for that reason it is worth having these few notes to hand, you cannot possibly remember to ask everything everytime.

I cannot stress enough that this is not a script to follow. It's a guideline, a checklist, a reminder, whatever you want to call it but don't just go through the same questions and points in the same order on all your calls. Be natural, this 'script' is there to help you achieve, not to limit you in any way at all.

21.1 Natural Language

If we look at the introduction format again and think of natural language you may think that you don't always get time to go through a full introduction like that and it might not sound natural. Do not be afraid, nay, actively seek to relax the introduction to suit your own style. That may well be a very useful and professional introduction but it's not going to work every time and if you did just read the same introduction verbatim, time and time again, you are only going to sound scripted and robotic, which is the last thing we want. Scripted and robotic is unprofessional.

Utterances such as, 'I wonder if you can help?' and 'hello there' aren't going to bring your introduction crumbling down, neither is missing one of the elements of the introduction, just get as many as you can in, being as relaxed as you can to sound more professional and less like you're going through the motions. This is something to be maintained throughout your call.

Be professional and be yourself!

Conclusion - The Business Relationship

And there you have it. How to get more sales. A lot of the ideas introduced in this book may have been things that you have done before but never realised were things that you did well, other ideas may be brand new. One thing that is for certain is that all the ideas shared in this book will bring your level of performance so far beyond that of the bog-standard 'cold-caller' you won't ever consider yourself to be doing the same job as them again.

Many more sales and many more business relationships begun. The important thing from a sales person's perspective is to manage this business relationship to order to produce more repeat business and referral business, the most lucrative source of work there is. You will probably have other people in the company that help to manage the relationship, field sales people, customer services, those who handle your delivery channels, accounts etc. However, don't lose contact with the existing clients because they can and will produce lots of business, whilst ever they are happy using your company and you are proactive in asking them for referrals. I think I said this earlier but – referral business is the most effective way to build your client base. Just thought I'd mention it again...

Appendix

Summary of Top Tips

Here are a few reminders of the key things that have been presented in this book. If a tip here is of particular interest, you might wish to look back to that chapter and re-read it. I have put the chapter number in brackets to help you do this.

I hope that there are plenty of new ideas here that you can incorporate into your calling.

1. *Be customer focused.* Orientate yourself throughout the call to consider things from the customer's point of view and get to know each customer individually in detail in order to find the best solution and best way of presenting a solution to them to increase your chances of a sale.

2. *Use your surname!* Simple and effective. Only using your first name makes you sound like a call centre worker, whilst using your full name (particularly as part of your introduction) sounds far more professional and will make the customer sit up and take more notice of what you are presenting (1.1).

3. *Speak to everyone with as much patience and politeness as you would the decision maker.* Just because they don't sign the contract or write the cheque doesn't mean that they cannot give you lots of useful information, guide you in the right direction and increase your rapport with that company (1.2).

4. *Leave a voicemail.* Leaving a voicemail for a customer you've yet to speak to gives you the opportunity to leave a full professional introduction so that the customer knows who you are and why you are calling and are expecting your next call. Strong prospects are likely to call you back (1.5).

5. *Make every call count.* Even if the decision maker is not available, always try to gain one extra piece of useful information from that call. Where they are for rapport building, when good contact times are to save extra calls and time, extra pieces of contact information so you can try a different route. These are all useful and something a colleague can provide (2.1).

6. *Email introductory literature whenever possible.* Emails are received quicker and are more likely to land on the decision maker's desk than information send through the post. Though there are problems with misspelling and junk filters, emails are cheaper, more versatile, environmentally friendly and time saving (4.2).

7. *Organise all contacts into groups.* This will help you remember where you got to with a particular call and help you prioritise the strongest prospects. Organising your data in this way helps you make more progress with each call as you are more focused on your objectives (5.1).

8. *Gather as much contact information as possible.* Quite simply, the more contact information you have for the decision maker the more likely you

are to achieve a sale as you can maintain flexibility in contacting them and stick to their preferred methods and times for contact. Aim to gather as much of this as possible on your first call (5.3).

9. *Make thorough notes.* Make as many notes as possible, what happened on the call, who you spoke to, good times to call back, any rapport built, any preferences expressed, opinions of current providers and so on. All of this is very useful for you in building the relationship. If you don't make the notes and you forget pieces of information on a follow up call you have taken a step backwards (5.4).

10. *Open with good open questions.* 'Tell me...', 'Describe...', 'Explain...', 'Talk me through...'. Journalist style questions that will bring the most out of your customer. Why ask, 'Who? What? Where? When? Why? How?' when one question will do (7.1).

11. *Fill in the gaps and focus on certain areas with fact-finding questions.* Any information not initially given can be explored further with these, more focused questions. Who, what, where, when, why, how (7.2).

12. *Call to action with closed questions.* Only ask questions that can be answered with a 'yes' or 'no' when that's the type of answer that you are after. i.e. at the end of the call. 'Would you like more information on this?' 'Could I call you closer to the time?' (7.3.).

13. *Rapport isn't just talking about the weather.* Rapport is gradual and is build through building trust, learning about your customer, maintaining professionalism, following through with promises made and is to be maintained with clients. Take time to maintain these standards in order to develop rapport (8.0).

14. *Avoid politics and swearing.* Bad language, political ranting and generally talking about yourself too much are things that will turn a customer off. Don't dominate the conversation or give the customer opportunity to judge you personally as not to weaken rapport. Keep it about them (8.2).

15. *Read the paper.* Being up to speed on current events in the wider world and your relevant business sectors will give you ammunition when speaking to other active business people. You will appear more informed and impressive when able to converse about such things (this does not include reality TV and celebrity gossip so choose your source carefully!) (8.3).

16. *Get a map.* Brushing up on your geography will help you connect and build rapport with people, particularly if you are calling nationwide. Think of how your local knowledge might help when you call somebody close by and try to expand that ability (8.4).

17. *Find the customer's key interest.* Every customer has favoured topics be it sport or other hobbies, current events or interest in a particular area of business. If they raise one of these, latch onto it and use it regularly when you contact them (8.5).

18. *Listen actively.* Make verbal acknowledgements when you are listening to a customer speak. This will show your interest, increasing rapport and encourage them to speak for longer. Make sure the acknowledgements are short and varied (8.6).

19. *Use lots of positive language.* The use of superlatives subliminally gives the customer a positive feeling towards you and your company. Great, super, fantastic, wonderful, brilliant, ideal, perfect etc, etc. Vary them, using the same one will stand out and make you sound inarticulate. Also avoid 'weasel' words that serve no purpose in your speech (8.7).

20. *Kill the weasel!* Try and stamp out those phrases which you habitually use over and over again. Keep your language relevant and varied. If you keep repeating a word or phrase your customer will pick

up on this and it will distract them from what you are talking about, hindering your progress (8.8).

21. *Know your apples!* Product knowledge is key. What more could you know about your products or services? Have lots of examples to hand and be able to engage with the customer on a technical level. Could you also know more about the sector you work in? (9.1).

22. *Know your competitors.* They would take business from you, given the chance so it's your job to take business from them. Know your main rivals and analyse their strengths and weaknesses. Highlight your benefits over a rival to get your foot in the door but *never* bad mouth anyone – it will only reflect poorly on you (9.2).

23. *List your USPs, features and benefits.* Introduce items from the list to your customer at the relevant time. Your unique selling points should be key business winners for you but show that you have quality throughout with your other business features which make you very competitive and always try to stay customer focused by highlighting the benefit to the customer (10.0).

24. *Present your benefits from the customer's perspective.* For instance, 'you can save money with us', has a lot more impact than, 'we can save you money' (10.3).

25. *Meet genuine customer needs.* Ask the question to check on the customer's situation and then introduce the benefit. Make what you sell appropriate to each individual customer and do your upmost to satisfy their requirements and you receive a huge boost in sales (11.0).

26. *Buying signals are earned.* Buying signals are not just sat at the other end of the phone waiting for you to call, you earn them through lengthy, quality calls. Don't be expecting buying signals after twenty seconds! Learn to identify the buying signals that occur later in the call (12.0).

27. *Look for long and short term opportunities.* Where can we secure the business in the short term? What are the long term possibilities for this customer? Both sides are vital for business growth focusing on just one will hinder business sooner or later! (13.0).

28. *Your existing customers are a goldmine.* When might they next need your services? Do they know anyone else who could benefit from your services? Two questions, that when asked of a satisfied customer equals a lot of new business (13.4).

29. *Personalise your sales presentation.* When you are ready to present your solution to the customer take ownership of the situation and personalise the solution by starting with the phrase, 'what I can do for you is...' (14.0).

153

30. *Give the customer choice*. An 'A or B' option is much more likely to secure a deal that a 'yes or no' option. There are several other closing techniques but this is very effective because you are allowing your customer choice unto the end (16.1).

31. *Keep motivated*. Find what drives you and focus on it. Pin it up near your desk. Whatever it takes because if you aren't motivated and positive on the phone your customer will tell and this will have a negative effect on your calling. You'll also make fewer calls. A sure-fire way of getting less business (18.0).

32. *Be on the phone more*. Yes make more calls but more importantly – make the calls count. The sales people who spend the most time on the phone overall secure the most business, not simply those who dial the most numbers. Ask more questions, develop the relationship, don't rush – the more time that you and a prospect spend speaking to one another, the more likely you are to secure a deal (19.0).

33. *Don't be scripted*. Have a script to hand for pointers only. Don't read from it verbatim. Be natural, flexible and confident on your calls. It is very easy for your customer to spot if you are engaging with a piece of paper on your desk more than you are them (20.0).

Things to discuss with your line manager/colleagues

Here is a checklist that you might require another person's opinion or authorisation on:

1. *Introductory literature.* Is this introductory information in the appropriate format? Is it flexible so that you can amend it accordingly to fit customer specifics? Are both spelling and grammar immaculate?

2. *Data Capture.* Is all vital information required accounted for in your database/CRM? Are there any useful fields that you could add?

3. *Notes.* Are the notes you keep sufficiently detailed that someone could make a call on your behalf when you were away and be fully up to speed on that particular customer?

4. *Weasel words.* Have somebody listen to your calls and identify any words that you repeat regularly, particularly those which serve no purpose. Examples, 'obviously', 'no problem', 'okay'.

5. *Research.* What publications would be good to read? You are looking for those which discuss topics of importance to your target market. Are there any

good times during your week that you can dedicate to research i.e. quieter times?

6. *Competitors.* Who are your main competitors both directly and indirectly? Perform a SWOT analysis (strengths, weaknesses, opportunities, threats) on your competitors and discuss this with your colleagues or line manager.

7. *Selling points.* Create a list of USPs, features and benefits for your company and get feedback on this to ensure you have as many as possible.

8. *Appointment feedback.* Ensure that any field sales person who attends a sales appointment that you have booked for them receives a briefing sheet as exampled in chapter 15.2 and that they give you detailed feedback following the meeting. This will help you improve the quality of the appointments that you book and you will also not compromise the contact with that particular customer.

9. *Existing clients.* Is there scope for all existing and/or historic clients to be contacted for an update to discuss their upcoming requirements and get possible referrals?

10. *Referees.* How many referees do you have in place, in what areas and how much business do they

generate for you? Is there scope for a campaign to increase the number of active referees you have in place?

Sales Articles

Please feel free to visit http://www.salesunited.co.uk for further details on the author and services available. Free sales articles can be received by entering your email address into http://www.salesunited.co.uk/articles.php, all articles are free and your email address will not be shared with third parties. Some article content is covered in this book.

Articles are emailed out approximately every two weeks. Here is an example:

Goal Setting

The start of a new year is the perfect time to set yourself goals and targets for the upcoming twelve months.

In sales, focus is key and making a commitment to achieve your goals rather than seeing what comes along will go a fair way to helping you boost what you bring in.

Take five minutes to go through the calendar and put a figure or two at the end of each month. These should be targets based around what you hope/expect to achieve each month (or week or quarter, whichever suits your business best) throughout the year. The numbers can be the number of appointments you are looking to get booked, the number of sales, the number of new customers, the amount of revenue you bring into the company or a combination of these.

Making these commitments at an early stage will stop you becoming content with a smaller number of sales by keeping your eyes on the goal and keeping you motivated.

If you are still building your business or yourself as a salesperson you may wish to take this opportunity to build up the number of sales throughout the year. However, I would advise that building up your client base and improving your closure rates etc can take time so don't be over ambitious with your targets for growth. Most managers will be happy that you are improving month on month so laying out a steady target for growth in your sales such as, January 20 appointments, February 22 appointments, March 24 appointments and so on, should suffice. This might not appear like much at first glance but it represents a 10% month on month improvement, which should please any boss and by the end of the year you could easily have doubled your monthly target from what it began at in January.

Being ahead – If you get ahead of your target during the month or year, do not let yourself relax, sales can be like buses, you never know when the next one might turned up whether its expected or not! If you find that you consistently meet your targets, look to the next quarter and think about adding another 10-20% in order to keep pushing yourself forward.

Being behind – If you see yourself falling behind in a particular month, worry not, the next sale might be right around the corner. If your targets are revenue based, one big deal can make all the difference. If you find that you have not achieved your targets for a few months, set yourself a safety net target (what you need to achieve) and a goal (what you would like to achieve). You will find that you will then fall into this area and subsequently feel more confident about pushing forward.

Do discuss your targets with your line manager, though ultimately they will be more effective if you choose them and feel confident that with focus and elbow grease you can achieve them.

Tony Pearson

The Open Question Misconception

Many sales trainers will tell you that there are two types of question. The open question and the closed question. An open question being a question that gets people to open up and talk and a closed question designed to draw a yes/no answer. They will tell you that there are 6 open questions – who, what, where, when, why and how, and even draw silly little diagrams of a large H with five little W's on – just in case you get stuck whilst speaking on the telephone and can't think of a question. You can look at your silly little diagram and suddenly regain the power of speech. And anyway – who, what, where, when, why and how – are not open questions.

Without wishing to belittle sales trainers (with their acronyms and pie charts) too much, let's just say that there's a lot they can learn from the world of journalism here.

A journalist interviewing someone of fame or other significance operate with the same initial agenda as a sales person – getting to know their 'customer' and extracting information from them. They just have nothing to sell them at the end so they tend to gather more information than the average sales person because they are not distracted by the ulterior motive – closing a deal.

So what is an open question?

An open question is a question that allows your customer to tell you the full story from just an initial prompt. A journalist knows how to ask one question instead of at least six (there can be more than one who's and when's etc in a situation).

The first question an interviewer will ask will usually begin; Explain... Describe... Tell me...

The interviewee can then open up to speak about the situation as they see it. The interviewer will then ask *fact-finding* questions to fill in any gaps – who, what, where, when, why, how.

How can this help my sales?

Imagine the impact of really allowing your customers to open up. What difference would the phrase, 'tell me about your ideal car' make to those sales that usually start 'what sort of car are you looking for?' 'erm, not sure' or 'how much are you looking to spend?'. Opening your customers up is the ideal way to understand their requirements (see previous article on Customer Focused Sales if you haven't already) and is key to building rapport. You then use your fact-finding questions to fill in the gaps, 'that's sounds fantastic, what colours do you prefer?' and your closed questions to close the deal, 'are you happy to sign today?'.

Try it...

Next time you are speaking to a prospective customer try using an opening statement (after 'hello' of course) that begins with Explain... Describe... Tell me... (avoiding Explain what... Describe where... Tell me who... as this defeats the object) and test this against on the next call/meeting against a who, what, where, when, why or how. I'm sure you'll find the results very pleasing.

And to any sales trainers who say it's not a question if it doesn't have a question mark – thanks for the input but we'll leave you to your diagrams and mnemonics and we'll have all the customers.

Tony Pearson

Articles are not training documents but more aimed to be shared best practice and to help generate ideas of your own. They are generally a one page document and can therefore not go into the level of detail found in this book. However, they could just be that extra piece of inspiration in your week. Article contributors are welcome, if you would like to share your ideas with other, like-minded sales people. Contact the author via the website http://www.salesunited.co.uk.

About the Author & Where this book comes from.

Tony Pearson is a graduate of the University of Sheffield where he read English Language and Literature. His wealth of sales experience varies from finance to fudge and security to pharmaceuticals. He works with many clients to help train their telesales personnel to work more effectively whilst enjoying what is one of the most important jobs in any company. Here's his story:

I have worked in sales my whole life. That for most means, from leaving school. No such gratuity for me. I had my first paid job at six years old. Yes, six! My Mother was a part-time Manageress at a local 7-11 and if my grandparents weren't able to look after me whilst she went to do her shift she would take me with her and I would spend four hours sat on the floor with a pricing gun pricing up tins etc. I was paid fifty pence per hour. Honest! At six money doesn't really mean anything to you but the two pounds a time went in my piggy bank and I was proud nonetheless. I just liked working, liked going places with my parents and being told that I was a 'good boy' for working and behaving myself.

Dad was a delivery man. He and my grandfather had a franchise in nationwide freight company. Dad's days were long, he'd leave at 6am and not get home until 7-7.30pm so I didn't really see much of him when I was at school, which is why I was so keen to go to work with him when I was seven, eight years old, during the school holidays. I would spend the entire day with him and get involved in everything. We would go to the depot and load the van, go out and do all the deliveries, have a bit of lunch in the cab, spend the afternoon doing all the collections from Dad's regular customers. What I always loved about the afternoons was how all the customers were with my Dad. He'd walk into a factory that he had to pick up from and people would shout 'Hiya Daz!' (his name's Darren) at him across the courtyard, others would stop and talk to him about football, the women in the office where he had to pick up his consignment notes would always have a big smile when he walked into the room and have something other than just the boxes he was collecting to talk about. Whenever he fancied a cup of tea, he could phone ahead to pretty much any client and tell them to put the kettle on and they would have a tea (with milk and two sugars) ready for him when he got there. I always found all this amazing. His didn't work for or with any of these people, his only job was to come in and collect the boxes that they were sending out each day, a two minute job in the midst of a busy afternoon and yet, every customer, without exception treated him like a close friend. At the time, I just thought that everyone loved my Dad like I did but it was only later that I realised that the reason they all paid so much attention to him was because he'd built up that relationship from scratch. He was a franchisee and so had to go out and build up the business in that area. He had sold to them and continued to deliver on his sale and maintain those relationships with people that led to more and more business for him!

I didn't actually have my first *sales* job until the grand old age of nine. My Mum hadn't worked for a year or two since the birth of my baby sister and we'd moved to Yorkshire to be closer to my Dad's business. One of Dad's customers was a greetings cards manufacturer. They would throw away any slight seconds or old stock, so Dad used his good relationship with that client and agreed to take away all their slight seconds free of charge. A win-win. My mum and I would then go to the local market on a Sunday and set up a card stall and sell all the cards. I hope at this point you don't think my parents were cruel, I honestly loved every minute of working with them growing up. It was here, at nine years old, selling greetings cards on cold Sunday mornings before my football matches that I fell in love with selling. Talking to people about birthdays, Christmas, weddings, anniversaries and helping my parents earn money was brilliant. Dad brought home different things, Mum's business evolved and from then on, weekends and school holidays were spent working across the country selling jewellery, gemstones, fudge, hats, coats, ornaments, badges, bonsai trees, flower arrangements, you name it, I've sold it! What I guess I'm trying to put across with all this is that selling became something I did quite naturally, as with anything you do from quite a young age.

I never realised that I was actually particularly good at selling, it was just something I did. Then, at nineteen I decided that I wanted a change from working with my parents and took a job in a call centre for a very large bank. I was still studying so I just worked evening shifts. After two months of training we were put on the phones. It was a customer service role, with sales targets for passing leads through for loans, mortgages, savings accounts etc. After just four months on the phone my sales were more than double the closest person from my same training course and I was placed on a dedicated lead generation line. I did that role for two months full time because it was the summer holidays before I went to University and during those two months I was fourth from 500 call centre staff for sales. The top three had been there for a few years full time and I'd done the equivalent of my first 4 months full time to be right up there! I was almost as amazed as the call centre managers who helped relocate me with a promotion when I left for University.

My degree is in English Language and Literature and I am fascinated by the intricacies of language. After leaving University I ran a business to business Sales and Marketing company, specialising in lead generation and appointment setting for clients across many sectors. My training and project management meant that over 90% of our contracts delivered targets and we had an exceptionally happy client base. The projects included freight and logistics, scientific and medical products and services, web design, security services, launching new, innovative products of all descriptions. The mission on the phone was always the same: find out more about the person on the other end of the phone and see if they would benefit from what you were selling. If this was the case then we would set up a sales appointment on behalf of our clients. Sound familiar?

We could never account for the sales abilities of our clients face-to-face or the absolute quality of their services and their overall competitiveness in their marketplace, a lot of the clients did exceptionally well from our programs, others couldn't sell food to a hungry, rich man but one thing was for certain, every appointment was qualified to be with a decision maker who had a good level of requirement for those services. Never once were any hit and hope appointments booked. My face-to-face conversion rate was comfortably above 50%, which is excellent going for business to business services and it was all down to the same techniques that I've walked you through in this book.

I've had several other sales jobs which have all added to my experience of selling both over the phone and face-to-face and I know how difficult people can find it to pick up the phone to make a sales call. I really enjoy sales and I particularly love picking the phone up and speaking to people. I hope this comes across in this book and that all my experience can help you get better results and enjoy your selling more. I now work as a sales consultant and help businesses improve their sales process with sales and marketing strategies, sales training, lead generation and project management. I can't wire a plug but I can sell and I'm a firm believer in sticking to what you're good at!

I wrote this book because during my career I've worked with, managed and trained people who have been decent sales people but missed out on excellent opportunities because they didn't ask the right questions, didn't have enough confidence to pursue a customer, didn't pick up on a buying signal, didn't have the motivation to make more calls and so on and so forth. I've been as guilty as anyone but by taking the time to pay attention to your selling methods, take new ideas on board and try them out and have more confidence in yourself and what you sell, hopefully this book can help you pay for that trip to the Caribbean, that new car or that pair of Jimmy Choo's!

Happy Selling!